MW01595669

Raising The Facebook Nation:
Stories Every Parent Should Hear

Raising The Facebook Nation:
Stories Every Parent Should Hear

Shawn M. Stewart, Ph.D., HSP

with: Annette Nole Hall

Stewart-Beavers Institute
2014

Copyright © 2014 by Shawn M. Stewart

All rights reserved. This book or any portion thereof may not be reproduced or used in any manner whatsoever without the express written permission of the publisher except for the use of brief quotations in a book review or scholarly journal.

First Printing: 2014

ISBN 978-1-312-57007-8

Stewart-Beavers Institute
PO Box 543
Brentwood, TN 37024

www.stewartbeaversinstitute.com

Ordering Information:

Special discounts are available on quantity purchases by corporations, associations, educators, and others. For details, contact the publisher at the above listed address.

U.S. trade bookstores and wholesalers:

Please contact Stewart-Beavers Institute
Tel: (615) 782-0504; Fax: (615) 782-0510 or
email: stewartbeaversinstitute@gmail.com.

Dedication

To my amazing wife, friend and partner in all things, Lisa.

Thank you. Without your support and patience, I would have never achieved my dreams. You are the reason.

Contents

Acknowledgements

Sometimes in life there are challenges, which define more than the immediate obstacle but they help define the person and their life. This book has been one of those experiences for me. This book represents the most pivotal period in my life, thus far, for many reasons. Two and half years prior to this book being published I had a "massive coronary event", or so the doctors called it. This led to the subsequent surgery and recovery, which happened during the initial phases of this book. Strangely this book took on more meaning than it had during the conceptual and early writing phase. It became necessary for me to enlist Annette Hall to help tell some of these stories through the fog of recovery and rehabilitation. It is with great appreciation I acknowledge her efforts and willingness to put up with my quirky creative nature and complex communication shortcomings.

For my family and "herd", I can't express in words the gratitude and appreciation for the level of support and kindness received through this process. It wasn't the big deeds but the small kind words and touches, which meant the most. It was the offers left untaken and the constant warmth and support for which I am endlessly grateful. I am a forth generation only child so my biological family is small, but my herd is great. These loved ones have carried me on their shoulders and accepted me into their hearts regardless of a reason why. We live by a philosophy that if we support each other the entire herd benefits. It has worked so far and for that my love and gratitude has no bounds. Rhonda and Cathy, Kristine and Micah, Colton, Levi, James, Rhea. I love and honor all of you as family. Blood it thicker than water but true friendship is stronger than steel.

To my immediate family, it is a small circle but one with which I literally couldn't have lived without. Mom and Dad – thank you for the gift of love and appreciation, for the lessons that carried me through and helped me not give up. Thank you for time and caring and all of the aid in so many forms. Sue and Swanson (who is no longer with us in person but inspires us from afar) – thank you for your support and desire to understand. For the visits and the caretaking. You were there in dark times and I appreciate the light. Pam and Greg, Kim and Junior – I never had siblings and have never known what that was like until you. Accepting me into your lives with reckless abandon and compassion as though I was there all the time. This can't be expressed in a way offering it justice. Just know I don't understand but accept this gift with all of the weight it carries. It takes my breath away.

Another true loss in these last two years was of Lisa's best companion Kobe, who during recovery was my inspiration and motivation. He pushed me and through his unconditional regard helped me heal. In his last days it is my hope that my aid and comfort to him was reciprocal.

Taylor, who didn't and still doesn't grasp all that was going on during her 4th year, it is my hope that turning your life upside down can have some positive effect on you and your growth. It is my hope as your dad that you forgive me for my absence and shortness, that you see my distraction as recovery and my sharpness as pain and not disappointment. I love you and am sorry you were the most effected by this.

Lainey – you were and have been my inspiration and driving force. As a father I have so much admiration and love for you and will always remember my workout partner during the roughest time in my life. I work every day to become a better person to live up to your example and amazing brightness. I ask your forgiveness for the distraction and not always being present to the fullest extent. You have had too much loss in your life and I work every day to be there for you and create a world deserving of you and your light.

Lisa – as I gaze at our wedding picture I can only apologize for not always being the partner and friend you deserve. It has been a long arduous journey, these last couple of years and I am so sorry for putting you through everything that has happened. You were there and picked up the monumental load at great cost to yourself and those relationships around you. The loss and grief you have suffered and the pain I have put you through is unbearable to imagine. I can only say that you are my muse, my guiding star and the reason for life to continue, Thank you all!

Preface

    This book is intended as a beginning of a conversation and not an ending point. Just as others who created the parenting concepts we use today never intended the conversation to stop but to continue as an open discussion regarding, arguably, the most important task society is charged, raising children.

    This book is also not intended to be a scared straight program triggering parents to pull back technology and hibernate from one of the most amazing times to be alive. In one of my past positions I was responsible for being the internal department IT guy all because I wasn't scared of technology and was willing to dive into a technology problem whether I understood the solution or not. My colleagues would often curse at their technology, "I hate this #*^%#$^%#$ thing". I got into the habit of replying, "It's technology, it is inanimate, it deserves neither or love, it just is". This is still true. It is technology and doesn't deserve fear or hated but respect for it's power and influence and a healthy appreciation for the tremendous damage it can facilitate and the awesome benefit it can provide.

    Take time and walk hand in hand into this technology journey with your children; the world will be a better place for it.

Introduction

There is no technology that is going to protect our children from all the unsafe sites, serial predators or cyber bullies they may encounter on the World Wide Web. Yet many kids have been turned loose, set free and given few guidelines to navigate their way through an unchartered frontier. We don't really speak their language. We haven't yet developed an ability to keep up or keep track with the changes occurring on a rapid and steady basis in their new on-line societies. But it is incumbent upon us as parents and educators to figure it out, because we are already are ***Raising the Facebook Nation***

We begin by looking at the old school model to examine the way we used to do things. Our study surveys the trends in parenting and education that have emerged in the last few decades by popularity and politics.

The book pushes it's way ahead of the pack to persuade parents, educational professionals and those in technology development to take a proactive position. It may be the only way not to be lost at sea while ***Raising the Facebook Nation***.

Chapter 1:

If it Takes a Village What Do We Do with the Crown Prince?

At first, she wasn't sure what she was seeing.

The images were distorted.

But she was curious and leaned in to take a closer look.

Slowly, the camera's view became clear…racked into focus…for her eyes-only.

Images so vile, disturbing, and violent, no amount of withdrawal, regret, dismissing, or distraction could ever erase them from her mind.

And even though she was safely behind the walls of her own home, she had been virtually assaulted in a way no emergency room rape kit could ever measure.

She was only eleven-years-old, just young enough to post her introduction to pornography on Facebook, but not quite old enough to comprehend the ramifications of what she was writing.

A psychologist by day, I wage war against destructive forces that do exist, despite all stages of denial.

By night I get to be a dad, debating how best to navigate the turbulent waters of technology in a world Christopher Columbus might have actually declared flat.

The synthesis of the problem is the old model. It was a good model. I mean Dr. Benjamin Spock wasn't crazy. He did his research. He knew what he was talking about. In 1946 his idea of a *"child centered"* home was a new approach, much appreciated, by those who had lived under a totalitarian philosophy of parenting. But 50 years later, with a sport utility of demanding and defiant children, we are looking for a society willing to share the responsibilities.

"With great power comes great responsibility," Spiderman said so himself. So how does this translate in an information generation where the focus, is *off* the family, and on the children? These are children whose abilities to operate every new piece of electronic equipment far exceed that of most parents. Yet they are children with underdeveloped minds and bodies in a minefield of cultural chaos.

Hillary Clinton didn't coin the term *"It takes a village"* but she did take the African Proverb to the New York Times Best Seller List. Times had changed. She was a successful working mother who modeled for other women the need for outside help. She pointed to the impact other people and societal groups could have on the development of a child's personality.

As a society, we sat up and listened.

Her nemesis, Bob Dole, the Republican Party Presidential Nominee shot back, *"It takes a family to raise a child."*

Clinton did not concede and books sales were strong. So were Dr. Spock's, reaching 50 million just two years later.

We were torn. Do we *"spare the rod and spoil the child"* or call on our communities to come to the rescue? There was one thing we didn't have to deliberate. We could protect the children! We were capable. We would and we could protect them. Despite specific parenting styles, this was a crossover. The most important piece to the parenting puzzle, at least for most Baby Boomers, we would stand guard, shield and shelter them.

In our culture, in our current society, we tend to draw the line of total protection, somewhere around middle adolescence, years 16 to 18. If we can protect our children long enough, if we can manage to keep them in a cocoon, protected from certain information, and let them reside in world of innocence, for as long as possible, we can take credit for the wonderful well-adjusted individuals they become. Then, our Parenting Plan, whether modeled by popular opinion or passed down in our own families, can give us a sense of satisfaction and reap rewards for our entire society.

In a perfect world it would work. But ours has changed. It continues to change. And change for us is inevitable.

The post 60's protected world in which Michael lived was warm and secure.

He was surrounded by all the niceties of a nuclear family in a homogeneous culture.

Michael's family ate breakfast and dinner together.

His dad was the head of the house and his mom made sure the family got to church on time.

But when he was only five years old, Michael sat at the kitchen table surveying all he could see and something didn't seem quite right.

Did this **Leave It To Beaver** world really exist outside the confines of his community?

Michael's parents were open in their discussions with him and his siblings.

They were open about *certain* things.

But there were some things the family just <u>did not</u> talk about.

Michael is my middle name.

Just because we didn't talk about the things that made my parents uncomfortable in front of their own children, didn't mean that I didn't know they were there. I was only five but I had a feeling someone was holding out. I saw things, I heard things, and I knew things. It's probably one of the primary reasons I became a psychologist. I knew very early on that there isn't a clear delineation between religion or cultures, gender or orientation, cultures and races. It's not as clear as people want. It's not dichotomous. And so even though I was raised that way, I knew from a very early age, that it wasn't right, that it didn't work.

I knew, for example as a young child, that there was this difference in the very core of Christianity that held our little family together. It didn't make sense to my five- or six-year-old brain that one religion, *our* religion, would be the only *absolute* religion.

My friends, who were accepted in my circle at school and allowed to come over to my house to play, were doomed to hell on Sunday morning because their parents went to a different church, the one that was literally across the street from ours. It didn't work. And it still doesn't work.

So I set out on a life-long journey exploring, investigating and analyzing all aspects of our need for continuous change. Change is hard. It is constant. It's a daring thing. I am an active agent of change, daring people to change when change is not just needed, but necessary. It's brought me to the apex of our current societal situation. We are now raising the Facebook nation and change is imperative!

Annie was only eight when she first heard the word sex.

She promptly went to her mom and asked what that strange sounding word meant.

Her mom, busied with folding laundry and clearly uncomfortable, told her to go ask her older sister. She never got a chance.

The three teenage boys next door told her first.

The things they described, the things they said her parents did, were never forgotten.

She was scared, confused and mad.

The worst part of all, she felt betrayed.

If there was something as horrible, as those boys described, happening in her own house, whey hadn't she suspected? Why hadn't anyone thought it important enough to tell her?

Annie's mom didn't tell her about sex because her mother had not told her. As ridiculous as that might sound to some who are willing to talk openly about anything, and see people do it on television every single day, much of our society is still struggling with the "when" to tell them. We are not so much afraid of the "what" but the "when" is still very much up for discussion. It's an ongoing debate that is causing division. Arguments are ensuing between husbands and wives, partners, parents and grandparents, school, school boards and PTA's.

Unfortunately while that talk continues, technology turns the timetables, and a moment of hesitation can be a life-altering opportunity lost forever.

The children who had parents progressive enough to have *"the talk"* are now asking themselves, *"Well, when did our parents tell us?"* So let's use that as our point of reference. Even though we know times have changed, that's exactly what we do as parents ourselves, we use our own time frame as a rough estimate for the time frame we are going to use with our children.

It won't work.

Any statistics I give you would be outdated by emerging technology before I am finished typing. But as an example, a 2006 study (yes, 8 years old already) conducted by the National Center for Missing and Exploited Children shows one in three children, ages 10-17 have experienced unwanted exposure to sexual material online. To be a little more specific, the material primarily included photos of naked people or people having sex.

Maybe you don't think your child, or the children in your community, are the ones who would necessarily be subject to such an eye-opening study. But where is our community? Our tribe? Our Village?

Where previous generations might have congregated at church three times a week, or accepted invitations for entire families to attend work events, things have changed. Less than half of us check in at church according to a 2010 Gallup poll and telecommuting is constantly changing Corporate America. School is now one of the few places we go on a regular basis to socialize with those outside of our own immediate neighborhood. School is often times consistent across cultures, genders, economic status; it's the one place we have, school. Now whether it's public or private, as they all differ from community to community, that's the one place we all share and congregate. We go there for school plays, school athletics, school events and PTA meetings. It's one place where we still get together. School is also the primary place where our children are actually socializing…or are they?

Eighth grade is believed to be one of the hardest years.

When you add preparing for high school to hormones and puberty; it's a stressful compound.

But for 13-year-old Jackson, moving to a new school was also a part of the plan.

A new laptop was enticing, cell phones were allowed and the 8th graders got extra hang time.

But he wasn't making friends.

It was unusual for him, out of character his parents said.

The school counselor became concerned.

Pressed for details, Jackson admitted no one was really talking to each other.

In the mornings kids were on laptops or texting.

On occasion a group would form to laugh at sexually suggestive cartoons on YouTube. But for the most part, at lunch and afternoon bell, heads were down and Wi-Fi was on.

Jackson found the electronic devices harder to penetrate than a campus clique.

And then they go home. If they have dinner together as a family, chances are they sit down at the dinner table together where everybody has their electronics out. They're either texting friends, checking emails or getting the latest stock market news. Although our children have never really known anything but a world full of techno-gadgets, we're modeling the behavior of what gets priority placement in our lives.

This is where I take some ownership for my profession and how it has impacted our current state of affairs. It wasn't done nefariously, but much of the technology we have in our hands was created in consultation with psychologists and sociologists. The idea was to create a situation where the tones, the types of tones, the information transmitted would promptly deliver a reward of immediate gratification. At some level, we're being trained by our electronics to respond just like a laboratory mouse.

You can train a mouse to run through a maze, click a bar and get food. Just as you can train a person to hear the tone of an incoming text message check it and get reinforced for *"Oh I've got new information that's cool."* We get immediate gratification, we get an immediate response, and best of all we get a little buzz of endorphin.

People who know what they are doing, who intend to draw us in by the technology, are the ones who designed it. Now ultimately, it's a marketing tool, the more you use the technology, the more technology you buy. The more you buy, the better the company. They're just trying to meet stockholders demands for an increase in the profit margin. There's certainly nothing wrong with that concept. It's the American way. But the effect on us is that we are being trained by our electronics, to be immediate gratifiers to technology.

The first day of classes Jackson was paired with a guy from the cool crowd.

The young man had volunteered to represent the school by showing a new kid around.

A few days later, Jackson had sympathetically gravitated toward some of the troubled children.

But then, in a quick turn of events, he was at the lunch table with the geeks.

When asked why, Jackson said, they asked me to sit with them; and I like that they wanted me.

The same principle translates to texting. Somebody wants me, somebody needs me, somebody is texting *me*. A lot of it is being chosen. It's a basic need. We want to be accepted. We want to be chosen. We want to be part of a tribe. We're genetically pre-disposed to operate that way. We get reinforced when we're more social, that is just part of who we are structurally, as mammals.

I go back to the old school rat running research. You can take water for a rat and use water as reinforcement. It's a great reinforcement because it's a primary need. You can add a light at the bottom of the water dish and the rat will choose the water with the light in it because it's more salient. It's more enticing. It's more exciting. If you add sound to the water dish the rats get really excited. It's got light and sound. Well now, the old water, which is still water, is not a good reinforcement anymore. If you take the other more enticing water bowls away, the rats will return to the regular water to survive. But given a choice, the bright shiny loud one is going to be a better reinforcement because it's more salient.

As adults, we follow along just as the developers knew we would. But who likes music and lights more than children? We allow the use of technology in schools, because educationally we have no choice but to keep up in our changing world. But it gives children a new choice we had not really considered: the student sitting across from them in the 8th grade hang time area at the middle school, or the new information coming in with light and sound? The electronic device is more salient than the person sitting across from them. That person has been there, and they know that person will still be there in a minute, right after they check this next text.

At some point the school bell will ring and any time for personal, face-to-face friendships, will be finished. But better yet, they can come home and make new friends on Facebook. Because in this salient driven society, many children are already trained to

gauge their social success, not by how many friends they have at school, but how many friends they have on Facebook.

Well, we're talking about kids 13years and over right?

It is a Facebook rule.

Allow me to shatter that little misnomer for you with a Consumer Reports study from the summer of 2011.

- Of the 20 million minors who actively used Facebook in the past year, 7.5 million—or more than one-third—were younger than 13.

- Among young users, more than 5 million were 10 and under, and their accounts were largely unsupervised by their parents.

Whether we like it or not, we are being forced to talk about things we have never talked about before. But in general, if you ask most parents, *"Do you want your children to be taught about sex in school?"* The first reaction is probably going to be, *"Oh gosh no, no!"* It breaches that line where we want to protect them. They don't have to know about these things yet. I think that is a human reaction, I think it is a reaction of the old model we used to raise children, a model we were raised with, and our parents were raised with, and the one that has been around for a long time. But, most importantly, that initial reaction we have grown up with has to change. The time frames we have imbedded in that belief are all wrong. If we continue to say we can protect our kids until age 16, it's not true. If you don't give them information until that time, they're going to get the information from very nefarious sources at ages 9, 10 and 11, and it's severe information, it's extreme information. So the model, the cocoon, has now become a prison. They have this information, but because we are protecting them, they can only handle the information in a protected way, which is internally.

I see children in my private practice who are on technology overload. We have to work with families on a regular basis to figure out where that individual line of too much technology is. Children have a threshold for technology and if they get too much it's like giving them a stimulant, they cannot shut down, they cannot relax, they cannot sleep. They are in overload mode. Their brain starts over processing information and they cannot stop. They cannot let it go. It happens all the time.

The study from the National Center for Missing and Exploited Children showed us one in three children, ages 10-17 has already experienced sexual material online.

Remember, Jackson's experience? When the children were congregating, it was to share some of the more salacious videos they could find, given the opportunity to surf unsupervised.

I have told you when I was only five years old I knew things were not so simple as this way or that. I knew my parents were protecting me, but I also knew there was important information that was being withheld.

It's a daunting assignment to develop a whole new model for parenting, for our schools, for our society. It's hard to change…it's a daring thing… but I get excited about the prospect of helping people change, even more so, when those who reap the rewards of change are the children.

Right now the soothing sound of chimes permeating the sanctuary of my comfortable office reminds me it is time to stop. We are already trained to wake to a bell, a buzzer or a song and we have long been trained to quit working when the whistle blows.

One more thing, let me just say, you know, Spiderman was right. *"With great power comes great responsibility."* Knowledge is power and we hold the responsibility to see to it that our children are not just protected by us, but educated about a new world, that reaches far beyond us.

Chapter 2

You Can't Stop a Tsunami, but You Can Move to Higher Ground!

She stares at the clock on the wall wishing she could go back.

She wishes she could go back and not see the things she saw.

She hopes someday her parents will forget she knows, the things she knows.

Her world has been restructured.

She is not an adult, but she has adult information.

The extreme images were things she wasn't ready to see.

They were things she had never heard about, never imagined, can never forget.

The crisis has passed, at least for now.

But every decision she makes will somehow be shadowed by what she saw.

Two boys sat and stared at each other in disbelief as their classmate engaged half of those sitting at the lunchroom table in the salacious details of his sexual escapades. Still not quite mature enough to shave for the first time, he was trying to convince anyone who would listen that he was having sex with his Christian-schooled girlfriend on a regular basis. The boys already knew about sex, so when the shock value fell short, he stepped it up a notch. As the holidays approached, he would indulge in *"MILF Monday, Tittie Touch Tuesday, Wack-off Wednesday, Thirsty Three-some Thursday, Fucking Fest Friday and Sexy Slut Saturday."*

They were intrigued.

But it wasn't until he bragged about his access to Internet porn and ridiculed his clueless parents that he had their full attention. On the way home from school that day, one of the boys told his mom all the things he had heard. He said he didn't really believe his classmate; but when he told her about the pornography, she could hear a hint of curiosity in his voice.

He had already seen Playboy Magazine at this grandfather's house, but what he had heard about between science and history classes could be accessed on his new iPad.

"Experience is a good school, but the fees are high." German Poet, Heinrich Heine spoke those words in the 19th century, long before educated minds could conceive the cost to a child caught in the 21st century's technological crossfire of innocence and overexposure. The fees are high. The damage is sometimes irreparable. We live in a society where evil is at our fingertips. As adults, we are often caught off guard, shocked, stunned, and embarrassed by what pops up on our computer screens. But then in blind faith, we hand laptops to our children, failing to recognize that it's not a lot different than giving a ten-year-old keys to the car.

Our post 9-11 world institutes every precaution against another terrorist plot when, in reality, our children are far more likely to be injured by what they are seeing on the Internet. And, as haunting as the image of a terrorist hiding behind every corner could be to the mind of a child, I suspect many of them have learned more about the threat of terrorism than about the potential dangers of surfing in cyberspace.

We have a problem. The solution will require change. We need a new model. Education *before* experience, when possible, will make the price less painful to pay. It's not unlike the model used by the Centers for Disease Control: **It is always better to prevent a disease than to treat it.**

In 1796, English doctor Edward Jenner discovered a way to prevent disease by preparing for it in advance. After recognizing that people who became sick with cowpox did not get smallpox, he proceeded to put the cowpox virus into a boy's body to help protect him from smallpox. It was the first of many vaccines developed over the years to help give us immunity to dangerous and deadly infections. What Dr. Jenner figured out was that his vaccine would imitate the infection and the boy's body would produce antibodies to fight it off. Once the child's body generated the germ-fighting tools then his immune system remembered what happened in order to protect him from another exposure.

The development of vaccinations has clearly changed our world. It was a new model. Change was necessary. Education before experience saved lives.

But then there are milder issues like colds and viruses where your body builds up its own natural immunity after being exposed to small amounts bacteria. Some experts even believe that parents, who disinfect everything their children come into contact with, may be doing more harm than good. According to the National Institute of Allergy and Infectious Diseases, a substantial increase in the number of allergy cases in the past fifteen years may be related to too much cleanliness.

I think one of the things we're doing with our children is trying to protect them from everything. We're overprotective; we're creating a situation where we have children who are raised in environments in which they are never exposed to certain stimuli. And, case-by-case, child-by-child, it is beginning to backfire on us. The new model begins with an increase of safe exposure. It's not in any way a bombardment of information too early or too soon, but gradually. Vaccines help our bodies prepare in advance to fight off infections and diseases. A safe amount of information will help our children prepare and then respond, in a healthy manner, to the things they may be exposed to in our new social media society.

Julie has three children who attend the same private academy.

One is in elementary, one is in middle and one is in high school.

When the school's popular coach was arrested for prostitution, it left Julie with a dilemma.

Her oldest child knew more than she did, since the news hit social media circles almost immediately.

Her second grader was fairly well insulated and she chose to keep it that way.

But realizing that word would soon filter down to the middle school she, knew she had to act fast.

Her middle child, a fifth grader, had never heard of a prostitute and had no idea what the word meant.

Julie chose to sit him down and explain it to him, educate him, before breaking the bad news.

Although somewhat stressed by being forced into such a position, she believes she did the right thing.

In the safety of their home, her son was able to ask questions and better comprehend what had happened.

If we have that communication early on, if we talk about it, children are able to process the information and adapt to what they are learning, rather than be psychologically injured by an onslaught of dangerous data. We have to address this type of issue through communication and education. There really isn't another option. Avoidance and denial hasn't worked, it doesn't work, and there is no research that shows it does.

Unfortunately, there are still those hedging their bets; and when given a choice, choose to react, rather than risk a proactive position. It's not just parents, but educators who know the power of information and still choose to hide from it.

Chad felt trapped.

He had known he was a gay since he was just a little kid.

But he had been raised in a strict religious home and sent to a very close-minded, closed-door school.

Not having anyone to talk to about this sent him deep into depression.

Eventually, he met others on-line who shared his feelings and secret relationships developed.

He was caught between the religious right and the liberal left.

It made him feel rebellious.

The girls, in whom he was able to confide, didn't share his fear of failing the people in power.

So they egged him on.

He wanted to confront his family and friends with the truth.

He even wanted the do-gooders at school to know who he really was.

When all attempts to broach the subject seemed to fall on deaf ears with family, friends and a guidance counselor, the girls concocted a plan.

Chad and his partner videotaped themselves in suggestive situations.

They posted the video on YouTube.

The YouTube video made its way to Facebook.

And everyone at school knew his secret!

Several months before Chad's secret sent shock waves through the school, the surrounding community and probably every dinner table on that side of town, I had warned administrators something like this was likely to happen. I told them they needed to get prepared. I actually said, "*You need to have a plan because this is going to blow up, and it's going to be a big deal, and it's a lot more serious than anybody thinks it is.*" I gave them the numbers, what we know statistically about these types of situations and what they were probably seeing among the student body at that particular time. In ongoing discussions with some of the students, I was seeing an emerging trend with the issue of homosexuality and how the school wasn't really dealing with it. I explained to school leaders what they were hearing about homosexuality in their school was only the tip of the iceberg. I explained to them that there was a growing acceptance among the students, where acceptance had not really been present before. It gave students the traction they needed. I warned them that their previous ability to squelch, hide or brush over such situations would no longer work. And in no uncertain terms, I strongly advised them to develop a plan, to be ready so they would not be forced to react. They did not follow my advice.

By not addressing it, the inevitable happened. It caused a tremendous uproar. The media started to pick up on it. It threatened to turn into a major news story, probably could have gone national. The students involved and their parents, and then all the students on the whole campus and their families, and the higher religious authorities all became involved in one student's exhibition of his sexual behavior.

Admittedly, it was the student's way of "coming out." This was, ultimately, a teenager's desire to be caught, confronted and hopefully accepted. But the firestorm had only just started.

It was the talk of every student. Every faculty member, every administrator, every maintenance worker and substitute teacher, everyone even remotely associated with the school knew about the video. Some were still trying to smooth it over, cover it up, say it wasn't a big deal when, in truth, it was a huge deal. The only thing you could count on was that everybody had an opinion. So then, at this point, we had some fairly young kids thrust into a campus-wide discussion about sexuality. Some of the students were prepared for it. Others were completely unprepared, but there was no way to avoid a head-on collision with all the scandalous details of the controversy. Students even started "FOR" and "AGAINST" pages on social networking sights. Students who were Facebook friends with all the other kids at school were being asked on their homepage, **"Are you "FOR" or "AGAINST" Chad?"**

The students who didn't want to choose a side felt bad because there was tremendous social pressure to pick. The ones who did pick a side often had friends who had chosen the other side. They were caught in a clash of chaos and confusion due in part to the school's refusal to have a plan. But, equally culpable were the parents who thought such things wouldn't happen at the expensive, private, Christian environment where they kept their children in a bit of a bubble.

I guarantee you, three weeks before this happened, there was a whole community of parents who thought they weren't going to have to deal with their children's inquisitiveness about homosexuality until college. They thought those would be questions left for later. The kids had seen enough on TV. The initial questions had been asked and answered and in no way did they anticipate dealing with the issue on such a grand scale. By no means did they expect the issue of homosexuality would affect their family so personally.

The first time the parents became aware of what was going on was when the school confronted them with their child participating in the Facebook poll. Again, we have parents hoping to procrastinate a bit on the higher education of homosexuality and, without warning; they are thrust into the discussion. Furthermore, they are forced into having a conversation about their child's choice on the social survey.

By not dealing with it and by not addressing it --at some point -- it's going to be in your face. Here were these helicopter parents, hovering over their children, placing them in a protected environment, refusing to talk about the tough stuff, enjoying their time in denial and then, all of a sudden, it no longer mattered. Facebook changed their lives. In a three-day period of time, all their plans to keep their children from the confusing and controversial complexities of life were suddenly brought to a screeching halt.

We are raising the first kids of the Facebook generation. They have got to have the tools to know what to do with the information they are receiving on a daily basis. Sometimes, they are actively searching for this information on their computers. But sometimes, it just comes crashing in on them.

And so the whole process of "What do you do, how do you do it, how do you handle it, how do you develop policies, how do you develop procedures," has to be addressed. The situation at Charlotte's school just turned into a mess. The information that was disseminated was not always truthful. There was no clarity. Many of the students felt the school's leaders were taking a hypocritical stance and kids were left with blame, shame and doubt. I think their reaction would have been different had this situation come out of the blue. But they had prior warning, and their response of "damage control" was absolutely unacceptable. When the people you trust tell you to have a plan in place and you ignore it, the consequences can be severe. And the biggest problem is students get hurt.

Further complicating the absence of a plan is a private Christian school that doesn't condone homosexuality, but also doesn't discriminate. So here's the problem. School officials were caught in a purgatory of sorts. They couldn't condone, but they couldn't condemn. It was in the student handbook. The school did not discriminate. But the primary reason it was in the handbook was because discrimination is illegal. So how did they handle it?

Remember, this is a Christian school. It has a church-based foundation with a board of directors that not only runs the school, but its members are respected in positions of leadership at their church. And, like many schools, especially those steeped in religion and tradition, those in attendance are often 2nd, 3rd and 4thgenerations. So when you have school leaders also leading the local church, and families taught to respect that leadership, there is room to operate outside the confines of the school campus.

Church leaders met with Chad's family. The magnitude of what his family was already dealing with, just by the manner in which Chad chose to come out, was immeasurable. But now, confronted by the very people they had been taught to obey since childhood placed them in a pressure packed position to make only one decision. When the meeting ended, everyone was in agreement; Chad would quietly leave the school. The school would be free of any allegations of discrimination because this was a decision made by Chad and his parents. There was nothing illegal about a family deciding this particular school was not the best place for their child. Further confirming they were making the right decision was the groundswell of support for the school. Over half the student body had sided against Chad in the "FOR" or "AGAINST" online poll of his coming out video. It wasn't unlike an employee leaving a wonderful job to *"pursue other career opportunities."* Most everyone knew, or at least suspected, what had happened behind closed doors.

So the students felt empowered at one level but disenfranchised at another. Chad left. The stories about why he left, lingered. Of course, as these things go, school administrators and teachers assured the student body that Chad left of his own free will and it was not due to the video, the poll or -- heaven forbid -- his confession of homosexuality. It was a mess of mixed messages.

It didn't end there. Long after Chad was enrolled in another school, the circumstances left behind continued to be fodder for debate. You can't really go to a Christian school, with religion and ethics classes, see school leaders sidestep the rules and then not expect students to bring it up for discussion.

American philosopher, psychologist and educational reformer John Dewey said, *"Education is not preparation for life; education is life itself. "*

I'm not saying your children have to know all things at all ages. What I am saying is you have to be ready in a moment's notice to address some of these hard issues because you cannot control what happens, what they learn from other sources, or what they are confronted with through social media. When given the option, we try to protect and shelter them from everything. The key is gradual exposure in a safe environment. It's not over-protection or under-protection. It's looking at the real threats and addressing them.

I've done crisis management: I've worked with kids who have been through tornadoes, fires and floods. But most of the children being brought to me for psychological counseling are not those experiencing natural disasters. They are instead suffering the devastating impact of exposure to unsolicited sexual material on the Internet. We need to be talking about it from the beginning, not waiting until something happens. Something is going to happen. It's already happening.

Michael was at his desk, in his bedroom, when he stumbled across some inappropriate stuff on the Internet.

As a precaution, his parents always checked his search history before bedtime.

When they recognized he had seen things he shouldn't have seen, they brought the hammer down.

Michael was blocked and locked out of every website that could remotely lead him into trouble.

At least that's what his parents thought.

He was allowed to visit a well-known website for an educational magazine.

But the study of extinct animals led him to an open forum and, once there, he was propositioned.

The person infiltrating the safety of Michael's home started by asking if he wanted to pet the animal's fur.

It escalated to requests for Michael to rub other parts of the animal's body.

Eventually the open forum's monitor caught the conversation and put a stop to it. But the damage was already done. You can't put that genie back in the bottle. Through all the net nannies, all the blocks and all the locks available, there really wasn't a sure fire way to control Michael's environment.

How are you going to block educational websites? How are you going to protect your child from Internet exposure? Most schools are now requiring a certain amount of work to be done on the computer. Many schools have already integrated computers into the classroom. Sure, parameters are put into place about the usage of computers during class time, but teachers can't possibly be expected to see every screen at all times.

Children who have been educated are in a much safer environment. They are going to be exposed to things, but, if they've been prepared, there's not that shame, guilt and doubt associated with not having the tools to deal with it. A lack of education and knowledge only puts them in a more vulnerable position than they are already in, just by virtue of being exposed to something they had not expected.

When a child is prepared and then exposed to inappropriate material, the communication lines are already open. The parent or teacher can step in and ask, *"What did you learn?"* *"How did that make you feel?"* *"Is this something you really want to experience again or can you let me help you understand how to avoid this in the future?"* Now we can move on. It's the same thing, at every point, addressing it in a safe way and saying, *"Okay, we got to preempt that situation by making you aware of all this information and letting you know, in advance, that it was going to be enticing."* It's much like the drug conversation that has happened on a national scale with public service announcements. You talk with your children and help them plan what they are going to say if someone trying to sell drugs approaches them. It doesn't mean they're not going to use drugs. It doesn't mean they're always going to say "no." But to have the conversation, being knowledgeable and preparing them, letting them know it is going to be there, helps rob the experience of the energy that it would have otherwise. It takes away the secrecy, brings it all out into the light of day and keeps the lines of communication open.

If you don't have that conversation, then what happens to them does get veiled in secrecy. There's things going on that you don't know of, you can't address, you can't help them plan for it, and you can't always repair the damage that is done after the fact.

Most people who end up addicted to drugs or alcohol weren't all that knocked out the first time they tried it. In some cases, the experience was very negative. Many of the ones who learned to listen to and then communicate after that first experience chose not to go back. It's like a kid who has a sip of beer early on and says, *"Oh that's awful! Why would you drink that?"* The first experience itself pushes back their follow up for quite some time. But when left to secrecy of what they did, combined with their curiosity and peer pressure, it often becomes "cool" and they push through the taste.

I'm not saying you have to give up all needs for control. But control is no longer about withholding something; it's about offering something. We must be willing to provide the education, before the experience.

The boys in the middle school cafeteria haven't quit listening to their friend's tall tales.

But now they do so through the filter of information.

The boy who confided in his mother was able to ask all kinds of questions.

She explained to him that some of his friend's stories might not be true.

Especially a story he told about using "double condoms" to protect himself.

The mom also explained that a young man who will disrespect his girlfriend and his parents would probably throw all his friends under the bus if backed in a corner.

They talked openly about what could be causing the young man to behave in such a destructive manner.

She also explained to him the hidden dangers of addiction when it comes to viewing pornography.

The boys still listen at the lunchroom table, but not as often or with as much interest.

Their new knowledge easily trumps all those stories. They're no longer shocked.

Chapter 3

No Child Left Off Line

A local School District, sent letters to the parents of students in grades 3-12.

A telephone survey would be conducted that night and parents were urged to participate.

An experimental initiative called "Bring Your Own Technology" was being expanded.

Students would be given a chance to carry their own digital devices to school.

This County is influential in the state.

So school leaders wanted parents to give them a heads up on what they could expect.

The telephone survey went as follows:

If your child does not plan to bring a device to school, **press 1.**

If your child plans to bring a smart phone such as an iPhone, Android or Blackberry, **press 2.**

If your child plans to bring a tablet such as an iPad or Android tablet, **press 3.**

If your child plans to bring a laptop, **press 4.**

If your child plans to bring an e-reader such as a Kindle or Nook, **press 5.**

Before his death in October 2011, Steve Jobs, Co-founder, Chairman and Chief Executive Officer of Apple Inc., fully recognized the power of the technology he had harnessed. *"Everyone here has the sense that right now is one of those moments when we are influencing the future."*

He also understood the magnitude of what was happening. *"We don't know where it will lead. We just know there's something much bigger than any of us."*

Technology is here. It will continue to advance. As school systems attempt to move forward at an accelerated pace, integrating technology into the classroom, the ship is still under construction, but we are already out at sea. Who will steer the ship? Which direction will it go? And how will it ever be completed, when the winds of progress are ever changing? These are questions educators will have to ask and answer.

Almost two decades ago, in his State of the Union Address, President Bill Clinton voiced the same concerns. *"We live in an age of possibility,"* he told a joint session of Congress and the American public. *"A hundred years ago we moved from farm to factory. Now we move to an age of technology, information, and global competition. These changes have opened vast new opportunities for our people, but they have also presented them with stiff challenges."*

In the same address, President Clinton advocated uniforms in public schools, if it would keep kids from killing each other over designer clothes. It was 1996. He had also vowed every classroom in America would be *"connected to the information superhighway, with computers and good software and well-trained teachers.*

Now, here we are in 2012, on the brink of voluntary initiatives like "Bring Your Own

Technology" to school and we run the risk of electronic devices becoming the new Air Jordans of the 21st Century. When the Williamson County technology story was published in the local paper, readers were offered an opportunity to comment. This was one public response:

"Even the wealthiest parents in this most snobbish county will not be able to buy iPhones and iPads quick enough to keep little Johnny connected. They will have to tie the devices to Johnny's arm with a Kevlar tether. Robbing school buses will likely become the most profitable business in the state."

Most people won't resort to stealing, but just about everyone will try to keep up with the competition.

"Oh you just have the iPhone? I have the iPhone 4S."

How much more pressure could there be on a kid in middle school? I experienced it in a therapy session right here in my own office.

A client in his 20's brought in his new Sony Vita. He was basically giving me a hard time because his technology was better than my technology. He was talking about it, showing me what it was capable of doing, showing it off, while all along comparing it with my iPad. It really was a kind of "one ups-man-ship." Client-over-Consultant.

Now, superimpose that situation on an 8th grade science class where "Bring Your Own Technology" separates the students on socioeconomic levels with a laptop. One kid brings in a new

MacBook Pro while another dusts off his dad's old Dell. Siri is looking up the day's assignment for a student on the iPhone 4S, while another student struggles with an old flip phone. Then, inevitably, a student walks into the classroom empty handed. What does that do to the hierarchy in the classroom? How does it affect the entire student body? What does it do to the mind of a child whose technology outranks that of the instructor?

Emily is in a middle school science class where the teacher is excited about her computerized learning tools.
She uses PowerPoint to illustrate the complicated scientific terminology she wants the students to learn.
Emily sits near the back of the class.
She has her laptop open.
She is pretending to pay attention.
She taps on her keyboard at the appropriate times.
Emily looks up occasionally and makes eye contact with the teacher.
But what she is really doing is emailing with a friend.
The boy next to her is playing an online game.
When the teacher hands out a pop quiz, Emily fails it.

PowerPoint would have been a great classroom tool back in 1996 when President Clinton was introducing hard-wired computers into the classroom. But graphics, animation and video have rapidly changed what is out there. The kids know more, and often have more, than teachers are able to keep track.

Even now, in the schools that I work with, schools where technology has infiltrated, rather than been integrated, I can't tell you how many kids are saying, *"I'm going to class, but I'm playing Words with Friends instead of paying attention to the teacher."* They're playing Minecraft or watching YouTube during class because they have teachers with lax technology in the classroom. So, then, who will retrain the teachers? And how will teachers monitor their students?

Allowing technology from the outside completely changes the classroom. The teacher doesn't have control over the content anymore. And the power shifts from teacher to student. In essence, the superintendent in the Williamson County School System prescribes this as a possibility in his letter to parents.

"Students will have opportunities to bring digital devices to schools, and they themselves will be asked to help identify the tools and strategies that will help them the most in their own learning. Teachers and administrators will work together to increase their capacity to differentiate instruction, teach students good communication skills, and extend learning beyond the classroom walls."

There's a shift in paradigms. And one of the things that will have to happen is a discussion about who will drive the curriculum. I think there's the post-modern kind of mentality, which is the paradigm that the students now drive the curriculum. Whereas, the old school paradigm is the intellectual academics and the folks who run the universities and the schools set the curriculum. I think it's a double-edged sword. Yes, it's good that students are starting to take some ownership. They can take on the role of driving the curriculum in their ideal direction, because they're integrating technology at a very core level. But their motives, in the use of technology, may be different than our expectations. It may be vastly different from the direction we need to go.

So from an educational standpoint, because technologies are so diverse and can be used in so many different ways, one student's direction may be purely educational but another student's may be primarily social, while still another student's motives are nefarious. If students are going to be the ones driving the curriculum, we have to make sure that we're adapting to it, so that we help structure it, instead of ending up in thirty different directions.

If we're going to use a post-modern perspective with students driving the curriculum, there has to be a process. We can no longer use an old school mentality of *"No, the administration sets the curriculum."* When school officials allow students to have all the latest technology, it pushes the students into the driver's seat and says, *"You're going to drive this, so where shall we go?"* What happens now is there is really nobody steering. We've got somebody in the driver's seat, and somebody who thinks they are in the driver's seat, and nobody has the wheel. We're not coming up with a good direction; we're not bringing it all together into a coherent package to define the curriculum. Yes, we want students to help drive curriculum and tell us what they need, but we also have to make sure there is somebody who is stepping back, from an educational standpoint, and looking at the big picture. It creates a huge challenge.

We are talking about a complete shift in the standard in the way teachers teach. Educators have pushed forward in the last couple of decades concentrating on teaching to the test. It's been driven from the top. There are people who develop the test. The test sets the curriculum. Teachers teach to the curriculum, which teaches to the test. When the students get the grades, it allows educators to say their schools are good. We've been training teachers to do that for 15 to 20 years now. Everyone is fairly used to that system. It works, it's measurable, and it can be displayed with bars, graphs and statistical analysis.

Now, we're going to completely reverse directions and, because of all this new technology, allow students to determine the types of curriculum. Teaching from that perspective is deferring, allowing the students to make decisions, and empowering them to ask the questions. It's almost a Socratic Method Approach. It's a mentality of, okay, we go back to questioning the students and having a discourse in the classroom, and having them push the direction of the class, which we decided about 15 years ago wasn't working. It didn't help us meet objective criteria then, so why will it now?

I see no plan of transitional education. There is no plan for what's going to happen, and no strategy for what we need to do. The Williamson County parents participated in the phone poll. But they didn't receive any materials on what the schools were doing to prepare, how administrators planned to manage the program, or how it would be implemented fairly on a system-wide basis. There was no information on how parents should talk with their children about the appropriate boundaries in a classroom setting.

Instead of bringing mobile devices from home, what happens when a public school system requires students to conform to a type of technology chosen by the school board? There are universities already requiring co-eds to purchase certain types of laptops. And there are private schools, where either parents are already paying the price for the latest technology, or an endowment covers the cost.

But a government-operated, tax-funded school system runs the risk of growing a whole new crop of problems. Superintendents and administrators are already talking about how a school system can traverse in such a competitive world. While it will require bidding and contracts, technology changes so fast, how will a system keep up while maintaining the integrity of the bureaucratic process? Does a school system buy in and then study the new emerging technology so that plans can be made for purchases in the next school year? Or, does the system let students choose what works best for them and adapt by providing platforms exchangeable between operating systems? I think different schools are probably going to try different options.

In the South, we tend to have a Chevy versus Ford mentality. *"I only drive Chevys. I'm a Chevy guy. And you're never going to catch me in a Ford."* Or vice versa. And we do that with technology. *"You know I'm a Microsoft person. I'm always going to be a Microsoft person. And I'm never going to use an Apple."*

Just like buying book bags or textbooks, will it now be part of an extra fee to purchase mobile devices for your student? And when a public school system requires parents to purchase a specific type of technology, so there is cohesiveness in the classroom, does that breed conflict? Who gets to make that decision? Are the parents powerless? Is it a popularity contest? If most school board members are PC users, is that the way it goes, or are students allowed to have an Apple because administrators want to move in that direction?

Do you require parents to buy a new Ipad for students every year? The technology changes every year. There is the Ipad, the Ipad2 and The New Ipad. Before this book goes to print, there will likely be more.

There are universities using new technology as a recruiting tool. Students are promised an Ipad or netbook as an enticement to bring them in and get them enrolled. Apple and Microsoft are all trying to create products that force the issue. College students can choose to go to different colleges, but public school students can't. They're going to whatever schools they are zoned to attend. And all requirements for the use of technology will be governed by a public entity; even though multi-billion dollar profit-making corporations may drive it.

Zach was a little apprehensive when his parents enrolled him in a new private school.

But the promise of a laptop/notebook combination seemed to ease his stress.

Although the school required the $1500 purchase, parents were assured it was good for three years.

There was even an IT Department with employees working round the clock.

The laptop didn't really work right at first.

But Zach was told it was operator error.

After several more visits to the IT Department, he just decided to use it only when he had to.

His mom's laptop was way more advanced and easier to use.

She only paid $1300 for hers and it had a much better operating system.

Still, like all the other students, he was stuck with it for the next few years.

Where does that leave Zach and the other students in two years when there's going to be six cycles of transition in the world of technology? New laptops, new notebooks, new iPads and who knows what else are on the horizon. But because the school system assured parents the $1500 price tag was good for three years, it's inherent upon administrators to honor their word. How does that impact the students? It depends a lot on emerging technology. Will their laptop/notebook combinations still be capable of adapting to new developments? Or will the students, who were supposed to be ahead of the curve, fall behind when other schools buy into the latest, newest products on the market for their students?

There are also the socioeconomic disparities to consider in each school, public or private.

As administrators at one school were planning for a recent trip to Washington, parents were asking if their children would be allowed to take along iPads so they could Skype. There was much discussion about all the different devices that would and would not be allowed. But then the talk quieted down when a mother, sitting near the back of the auditorium, asked if it was okay for a student to go without a device. If you can imagine, in this day and time, a teenager, on an out-of-state school trip, with classmates carrying the latest in technology, travelling without the use of a basic cell phone. It happens. There is still a divide that school systems may not be able to bridge regardless of the technological decisions that are made.

In this County where the "Bring Your Own Technology" initiative is underway, students who don't have an electronic device will be able to use an in-house supply of laptops and iPads. Do you think kids will know the difference? Will it be a little like the children who received free milk and government subsidized lunches back in the 60's and 70's. Will a child's social success be dependent on accessing a mobile device from home or being forced to use one that belongs to the school?

Those who can contribute will be expected to do so. And there are already organizations trying to get technology into the hands of students all across the country that can't afford it. Most are operating on government grants. But does that grant application involve re-upping every time there is a new technology cycle? And what happens six months from now when a student gets better technology than a student who was given assistance six months ago?

What message does that send? And how does a school system deal with it?

When Habitat for Humanity volunteers go into a neighborhood and build a house, they don't come back six months later and build a bigger house. They certainly don't come back in a year and build a mansion because developing technology allows them to build more for less money. Habitat volunteers build the same or similar houses, side by side, so they are all part of a community.

It's hard to do that with technology, because eventually technology disappears. What happened to VHS players? When was the last time you stopped into a movie store? How many people have already replaced giant desktops with small lightweight laptops? Whatever way we choose to bridge the divide, we're going to have to get to the point of intensive technology literacy.

In 1996, after President Clinton vowed to give every public school access to the Internet, I was among a group of researchers commissioned through a U.S. State Department grant to determine if it was a good idea. Our job was to go into the classrooms that had been hardwired for computers, with teachers trained, and measure the impact of technology. We had a very structured way of collecting the evidence and, once completed, we were to meet with our results.

I remember going into the classroom and watching the kids using the computer for the first time. They loved it. They were having fun. They were using on-line examples and doing research on their projects. The teacher had them go to a more project-learning curriculum, where they were integrating the technology in a full school year to learn everything they could about one topic. Their topic of the year was sea life. So they were learning about whales, sharks, sea snails and the like. They integrated it into math, science, geography and every other subject, until the end of the year, when they presented a finished project.

The students also had a sister school in Russia on the Internet; so they would exchange emails with Russian students their own age. As researchers studying the use of this new technology, we were thinking this is great! The teacher is doing an excellent job, the kids love it, and this has to be a good thing.

But in every objective measure related to learning we looked at, it was a bad idea. Every researcher came back and told the same stories... this is awesome... this is cool... we love it... we wish this was our classroom when we were in 3rd grade... but they're not learning as much. What we discovered was that technology at some level interferes with the quality of learning. Technology time was not necessarily quality time. Two things were affected. Two of the top predictors of learning are quality of time on task, and time on task. How long are you actually engaged in a learning activity, and what level of engagement do you have? And what we found was, in using technology, it took more time than old school paper and pencil and drawing on a chalkboard. What was happening before computer access, was a teacher preparing a lesson, delivering it to the children by paper and pencil and them receiving what she taught. What we've done with technology is add on more layers in the middle of the learning.

So we all met as a research group and told the representatives from the State Department that we loved what we saw, but we were going to have to report at that particular time that it was not a good idea. We explained that until we figure out what we're going to do, and how we're going to shift the entire way of learning, and figure out a way to shorten the time, and to increase that engagement, it's an interference; a cool interference, but an interference.

But the Department of State representative said, *"Sorry, you can't say that."* We walked out and our research was packed up and taken away. And so, instead of releasing our results as groundbreaking research, a book was published highlighting what the teachers were doing with computers in their classrooms.

Rapidly changing technology is leading us on a potential collision course in cyberspace. The World Wide Web is taking us places we may not be prepared to go. But we will go. The journey is already underway. We have only the option to look backward, see how we got here, and try to make the best decisions for our children's future. The charismatic pioneer of the PC revolution, Steve Jobs, ended up dropping out of school. Because of his success, he was asked to deliver the commencement speech at Stanford University, June 12, 2005. His words offer advice for ships still under construction but already out at sea.

"You can't connect the dots looking forward; you can only connect them looking backwards. So you have to trust that the dots will somehow connect in your   future."

Chapter 4

BEWARE:

The Information Super Highway

No Speed Limits and No Stop Signs

Most parents were at home when they answered the County phone survey.

Those who were attending school functions that night could not participate at the time.

Despite a broad invitation to "Bring Your Own Technology" to school, there was a bit of a problem.

Parents using cell phones could not get a signal on school property.

It wasn't an accident.

It was a blocker put in place to prevent the use of cell phones by students during school.

The 4th grade girl with the pixie haircut and freckles sat at the last desk in the third row.

She was new to the school and hoped no one had noticed her.

But then a girl with long blonde hair passed her a note from a dark-haired boy across the room.

"Do you like me? Check yes or no."

It was 1970, and that's the way it was done.

The 8th grade boy came home from his 2012 class trip and logged on to Facebook.

Two girls at his school were conducting a poll.

Should one of the girls give him a chance?

Check "Like" if your answer   is "Yes."

Many of his classmates had already offered their opinions before he ever saw the post.

One of the most quoted concepts in corporate America is *The Peter Principle.* It's the belief that employees tend to rise to their level of incompetence leaving most of the work for those who haven't yet attained advancement. Laurence Johnston Peter, a doctor of education, left our world with that nugget of wisdom, as well as other warnings on how quickly we can get ahead of ourselves. *"America is a country that doesn't know where it is going but is determined to set a speed record getting there."* And, *"If you don't know where you're going, you will probably end up somewhere else."*

In 1996 we knew where we were going. As a nation, we were moving in the direction of new technology that offered us an option to protect our children from overexposure. It would come in the shape of a V-chip; and the signing of the Telecommunications Act, which d all television sets at least 13 inches in size, be equipped with the device. It was designed to give parents control over the level of television violence to which their children were being exposed.

"If every parent uses this chip wisely, it can become a powerful voice against teen violence, teen pregnancy, teen drug use, and for both learning and entertainment," President Bill Clinton told his captive American audience as he signed the bill into law. *"We're handing the TV remote control back to America's parents so that they can pass on their values and protect their children."*

The United States Congress fell in line and decreed that the television industry create a way of rating their shows. Then the V-chip would be utilized to block programs based on how they were rated.

It was a great idea and gave us a renewed sense of security in a country that had been plagued with a series of unexplained school shootings. But it never really caught on. Some parents didn't know how to use it. Others didn't want to use it. And on occasion, those who did use it found out their children knew how to override it by simply reading the users manual and reprogramming the password. While adults do design and develop much of the new technology, the kids are frequently the ones a step ahead when it comes to utilizing it.

The lack of a comprehensive solution is an area so crucial to the healthy development of our children that we cannot afford to be outdone. I recently met with an Internet app specialist. An app is short for web application in case you are among a shrinking population of people who haven't yet downloaded one to your phone, tablet or laptop. And basically, it's a quick way to get you where you want to go for the things you need.

So I meet with this guy and told him the general concept I have for a more passive way to monitor all the different sites, text messages, emails and social networks children visit by accessing one app. Basically, what we have right now is blocking software tied to a browser. There are about five out there you can download for free. But then all a kid or a teenager has to do is upload a new browser and all the blocking software you think is protecting your children no longer works for you.

The problem, from his perspective, there is no really good technological way of limiting a child's access to anything and everything. With so many programming variations, and choices for content from websites, apps, text messaging, email and more, the challenge of designing a software shield is monumental. Add in the complexities of various delivery systems, whether wired or wireless, multiple Internet providers, phones, tablets, desktops or laptops, and the obstacles to overcome are even greater. Now bring in the free market with proprietary systems from Apple, Samsung, Toshiba, Sony, Android, Blackberry, and on and on, and you can see a technologically tangled conundrum that would cause a major migraine for even the most talented of programming geeks. The only way to do it, according to my cyber source, is to have a singular device and "jailbreak" it, which basically means opening it up and installing your own software. In doing so, you break the warranty. And, of course, you're told not to do that by the manufacturer. However, if that's the route you choose, you can secretly imbed monitoring software, which would be done in secret, so that it gives you the ability to find out what transpires on that particular device. You'll need to make arrangements with a monitoring company to send you a report of all the information flowing through the device you choose to "bug."

It's a little exhausting just rehashing all the reasons why it won't work. There are plenty of products available to block certain software, but not one central portal where parents can monitor all their children's activities. It boils down to one basic reality check. We can't rely on technology to protect our kids because there is none. The proliferation of the technology has blown the doors off any attempt to respond. It's gone too fast, we are way too far into it. It's entrenched in everything we are doing and we have failed to throw up any sure safeguards in the process.

I remember working with one mom whose son had downloaded child pornography and then sent it to another kid. I repeatedly told her to go to her service provider and ask them for help. She kept coming back saying she had been there, talked with representatives and there was nothing they could do. I insisted there had to be something that could be done. So finally, she learned how to open the phone herself and embed pirate software that could secretly monitor the phone. Of course, she did forfeit the phone's warranty but at least she had more of a handle on what her son was doing and just as importantly, what he was seeing.

Taylor is just four years old but she is already the envy of many teenage girls.

At gymnastics competitions, Taylor's parents allow her to bring her new iPad.

It doesn't have Internet, but it does have a game called Cut the Rope.

Taylor is good at that game.

She is so good the older girls want her to get on their tablets and help advance them in the game.

Although Taylor doesn't have access to the World Wide Web on her own device, the older girls do.

Her parents watch from the bleachers convinced they have set up appropriate safeguards.

But when will Taylor venture away from the safety of her game and out onto the Information Super Highway?

Taylor is my daughter. Her mother and I allow her to have access to her iPad during competitions because there is so much "down time" between sessions. We believe it's a good use of the technology to spend that time on something educational and mind stimulating rather than just wasting away a big part of her day. We also want to keep her focused and concentrating on something other than an opportunity to cut up with the other kids and get into trouble. She is four. And at four, we can keep a pretty close eye on her and make sure she's not venturing out further than she should. But up in the stands, away from the gym floor at a large competition, our ability to watch her every move, especially when she picks up an older girls electronic device, is impeded by distance. It will only get harder to keep an eye on her, as she grows older. So we are taking the proactive approach I continue to advocate. We are having conversations with her, conversations that are necessary even at such a young age. We are talking openly about the risks, where to go and what to do, and how to use computers responsibly. Taylor is learning how to use other people's technology, what is appropriate and what isn't. We have to play offense. The price of waiting until something happens to implement a plan of defense is just too high to pay. But there are still plenty of parents hedging their bets.

The whispering among teachers at school was similar to what some 3rd graders had witnessed at home.

Everyone seemed to be talking, but no one wanted to tell any of the kids what was going on.

Nicholas overheard that a friend's dad had committed suicide.

When he pressed his parents for details, they quickly changed the subject.

He asked his homeroom teacher and she told him to go back to his seat.

So Nicholas got a group of his friends together at lunch and they decided to find out for themselves.

They did what most any adult would do when looking for information.

They Googled, **"Suicide."**

They saw more than they ever expected.

No one wants to talk with their 3rd grade child about the graphics of suicide. We once lived in a world where most children were much older before they were confronted with such harsh realities. But technology has changed our ability to hide. It's changed our ability to put off until tomorrow what the children are going to find out today. We have to know where we are going.

Nicholas and his friends are now dealing with more than the details. Many of them can't sleep at night. They are having nightmares more often than most kids their age. The images they see in their minds are pictures many grown-ups have never seen.

The teachers at Nicholas's school, as well as the 3rd grade parents, couldn't even protect them from the details of the dad's suicide. He was well known in the community and his death was news. They found out exactly what happened, because they were curious and they had access to information.

So as educators and parents, here is a perfect opportunity to ask what we should do. It's fundamental. We have to change everything about the way we educate our children. We have to change the way we parent them. We have to change what we are willing to teach them and when we are willing to do it. Otherwise, they are going on ahead and going on without us. The option not to talk about it, when a child asks about suicide, sex, school shootings or whatever the topic, is no longer a viable option. As adults, we have to make the right choices. Are we going to control this flow of information or are we going to let them Google it? Are we going to help ease them on to the entrance ramp of the Information Super Highway, or are we going to allow them to be forced into oncoming traffic? As a psychologist, who counsels these children, I would rather see a parent or teacher sit down with a child and Google these tough topics together, than to see them risk irreparable harm to an inquisitive child. I wouldn't necessarily suggest looking up images unless you believe the child is going to do it on their own. In that case, I strongly recommend you choose to be there and help them navigate. It may require you to be a little more tuned in to what they are seeing and hearing. Most importantly, what are they asking? Where will they go for information if they don't get it from you? We can ease them into an education, like releasing pressure from an overfilled balloon, or we can ignore it, let them drift out there alone, and only react when the balloon bursts. It's a choice. It's a tough choice. But we are the adults. We are the educators. We are the authors of this time bomb of technology.

Two girls, only two years apart in age, grow up in the same house.

The oldest daughter likes to read but rarely asks questions.

The younger girl is quite inquisitive and her parents never really know what she might ask next.

But they rarely talk to the girls because, quite frankly, their parents never talked with them.

The older child grows up and has her own family.

She doesn't talk with her children about intimate topics.

She even lies to them when their pets die.

Her younger sister also marries and has a family.

She takes the opposite approach and talks to her kids about everything.

Some people think her children know too much, too soon, but at least she was the one who told them.

She's also the one her older sister's children come to when they have questions.

They know she will give them honest answers and they don't have to go to the Internet.

It's controversial I know. It's going to freak some people out. It's the parental divide we must find a way to narrow. No matter the recommendations, some people will not want to broach subjects with their children that make them uncomfortable. Still others are willing to tell their children so much, the kids could educate all their friends if given time and chance. But out here on an ocean of opportunity, to gather any information they choose, children are no longer willing to wait for parents to come around to their way of thinking. They want answers. We are out of options. We either give them the information they are seeking, in a controlled situation, or we try to repair the damage done when they go it alone. I don't see another option. Sex therapists, psychiatrists, child psychologists, medical doctors...other experts in various fields of study, whom I talk with on a regular basis, see no other options. We've got to move forward into the age of information. It's happening with or without us. We are parenting digital natives. These children were born into a time of technology. We have to learn to respond to their needs over and above our generational discomfort with information.

There will be no sugar coating of the facts on Yahoo, Google, Wikipedia, Ask.com or any other website you can search for information. The sites aren't designed to differentiate between what is and what is not age appropriate. There is no App or V-chip that is going to keep a determined child from finding a way to access information.

Jacob's mom found his phone next to the television while he was taking a shower.

She decided it was a good opportunity to check his messages.

As she started to scroll down through the most recent texts, she found several to a young girl.

Jacob's mom had adamantly forbidden him to text girls.

When he came out of the shower, she told him he had lost his phone privileges for the next week.

At lunch the next day, Jacob told his friend Noah what had happened at home.

The boys had already been discussing a time when Jacob could come over to Noah's house.

So, as far as they were concerned, the problem was solved.

Jacob could text the girl from Noah's phone.

Noah's mom didn't care.

And Jacob's mom would never know.

Sure, children of our generation used to visit a friend in order to sneak out at night, watch a television show they shouldn't or call a girl from a back bedroom telephone. But they could not carry on a real-time relationship via instant text message, talk to strangers in virtual chat rooms or access Internet pornography. This is a new frontier. We can't shy away from the reality of what we are facing.

A new model of parenting and educating is essential. As we begin the process, we can at least use what we already know. The way we talk is crucial. Even though a new language is being thrust upon us by constantly changing technology, we need to use correct terminology already in our vocabulary. Certified Sex Therapist, Dr. Lisa Beavers, makes it clear to her clients that the proper use of real words, rather than slang or lingo, goes a long way toward educating children.

A recent class assembly of teenage boys about to be promoted to high school is an excellent example. The young men were taken away from their laptops long enough to watch a six-year-old video about sex education. After final credits rolled, the football coach stood up to further explain what they had just seen. *"If you do anything with a girl that involves your wee wee,"* he told them, *"that would still be considered sex."*

These were 14 and 15-year-old boys, some already sexually active, not just amused by the coach's choice of words, but certain he had nothing to tell them they didn't already know. He lost their respect and as a result, they were no longer willing to listen. We have to equip children with information they can use. We can't dance around terminology when it's a click away. Like many other experts in her field, Dr. Beavers believes clinical terms should be used with children from birth. *"We've advocated it for many years and proven that it empowers them in situations where they might need to describe a problem to a doctor. But in this technology driven time, it also gives children the tools essential to help explain something they might have seen on the Internet."*

An open and honest conversation with a child, using the correct terminology, is not easy for everyone. I counsel parents who struggle to get through a basic conversation at dinner with their teenagers or young children. But having access to an entire world through a smart phone, tablet or laptop, forces us to take on the responsibility whether we like it or not, whether we are comfortable with it or not, whether we know how or not.

It's a global issue. It's as relevant in the Republic of China as it is in America, as it is down under in Australia. Parents, educators, designers and inventors bear a burden of responsibility when it comes to preparing children for what they may face on the World Wide Web.

It's just as important in impoverished countries, where children have to travel to the nearest town to find a computer, as it is in the wealthiest of locales, where purchasing the hottest new electronic device is a way of life. What if I'm in rural Mexico and we don't use technology, we don't even have cell service, but my kids go into town and go to the local computer bar? What are they going to be doing? What will they see? Who will they talk to? Are they prepared? We may be addressing it first, but it's already an issue in most parts of the world. It's happening in the UK, across Europe, in South America, it's everywhere. The Information Super Highway will claim casualties if precautions are not put in place. A new style of parenting, learning a language we don't really know, allowing educators more room to open up discussions, and taking proactive, rather than reactive, positions are all part of what it will take to raise this generation.

A new model may be out of every parent's comfort zone, but in the words of John Kay, front man for the rock-n-roll group Steppenwolf, *"Success at any price, demands its sacrifice."* Although known for his legendary hits, "Born to be Wild" and "Magic Carpet Ride," John managed to raise a successful daughter while performing concert venues all over the world.

We have to be willing to make some sacrifices, to make changes, to act sooner rather than later, and talk more openly than our parents and grandparents. If we just stick with the concept of *The Peter Principle*, we will simply rise to our level of incompetence as parents and leave the work of raising the Facebook Nation to someone else.

Chapter 5

The Push and Pull

Learning New Rules of Engagement

The smart phone started vibrating on the nightstand while Steve was still in bed.

His wife watched as he jumped up, grabbed it and went to work before a shower or even his first cup of coffee.

She knew he felt it was necessary to return text messages and emails to his clients and employees.

But it seemed a little invasive to her.

This was their bedroom and this was their time.

At dinner that night she got a text and quickly returned it.

It was her sister wanting to share a funny family story.

Steve didn't think it was necessary to text back at the dinner table.

It seemed a little intrusive to him.

This was family time.

When Steve looked over at his son, he was also texting.

Four girls from school were taking turns sending him messages.

He was trying to return each text while simultaneously eating his salad.

It might seem perfectly productive to some people.

But in this family, it ended in an argument.

Technology, in all its various forms, is changing our world, our lives and our relationships. We may be communicating more, but we are talking less. *"Cell phones are a mixed blessing to American families, bringing safety and connection along with disruption and irritation,"* according to The Pew Internet & American Life Project. It's one of seven projects that make up the Pew Research Center, a nonpartisan, nonprofit "fact tank" that provides information on the issues, attitudes and trends shaping America and the world.

It may be easier to work from home, but we're always working. And even though our children are part of a new social network, a form of communication that no longer requires them to talk is compromising their social skills. When surveyed by Nielson, teenagers said texting was faster, easier and more fun than talking. How many teenagers wouldn't prefer to text their parents from the next room, rather than engage in a face-to-face conversation? It's faster, easier and more fun than talking. They've said it themselves.

They've also seen the new communication style modeled for them at home and at school. And they've been witness to some of the confusion. This is an email sent to parents from the Dean of an exclusive private school:

Since returning from break, we have fielded multiple requests for students to bring in e-reading devices (Nooks, Kindles, iPads, etc.) to use during the school day. Last week, I asked the students to keep these devices at home for the remainder of the school year. These devices are valuable tools and a great platform for enthusiastic readers, however, at this point, the administration believes it is best that they are utilized outside of the school day. This spring, we will

be reviewing our technology and electronic use policies to determine the viability of allowing these devices on campus next school year.
Thank you for your support in this matter, and please let me know if you have any questions or concerns.

At the bottom of the email, below the Dean's signature were the words, *"Sent from my iPad."* The irony was not lost on the parents or the children. In the Dean's defense, the email was apparently sent from his home. But, in an age of instant communication, we are facing an imminent breach if we don't adapt and quickly respond to the communication changes technology is forcing on our families.

"What's not so great is that all this technology is destroying our social skills.

Not only have we given up on writing letters to each other, we barely even talk to each other.

People have become so accustomed to texting that they're actually startled when the phone rings.

It's like we suddenly all have Batphones. If it rings, there must be danger.

Now we answer, "What happened? Is someone tied up in the old sawmill?"

"No, it's Becky. I just called to say hi."

"Well you scared me half to death. You can't just pick up the phone and try to talk to me like that.

Don't the tips of your fingers work?"

— *Comedian Ellen DeGeneres, Seriously...I'm Kidding*

The downside is that all of us, but especially our children, are engaging in technology when they could be talking. The upside is, they are engaging in technology, to communicate with each other at times they, otherwise, might not be talking. A teenager, celebrating a birthday on Facebook, can experience a day that would rival having a pony at the party a generation ago. Well-wishes from three or four hundred *"friends"* can make you feel pretty good about yourself, at any age. But when you are just beginning to develop a sense of self, being propelled into the center of such overwhelming attention, can certainly alter a personality still in the developmental stages.

Kids are also communicating in places where talking used to be taboo. A running dialogue transfers via text between study groups in the library. A quick trip to the bathroom, during class, and a student can text a parent to bring a paper accidentally left at home. And then there's the new ability to deal with all things awkward through a social network.

I had a session with a kid in high school and during our discussion he started texting.

"Who are you texting?" I asked him. *"And better yet, why are you texting during our session together?"*

He said, *"I've got to, man. It's the girl we've been talking about."*

"So what is she texting?" I asked him.

"She said we have to talk."

You don't have to have a Ph.D., to know when a woman says, *"We have to talk,"* the topic at hand is very serious, at least to her. But this young man just planned to wait and find out what she wanted the following morning.

"That would drive me insane. I would have to know," I told him.

"Yeah, but if I actually text a response, we'll end up going back and forth all night. She'll never tell me until tomorrow morning anyway, and the back and forth is what will drive me crazy for the rest of the night."

Via text, he's pretty savvy. He's got the dynamic between him and his girlfriend figured out. He's learned, with this new technological tool, how to minimize the drama and keep the relationship going without hurting anybody's feelings. I thought it was very emotionally advanced for him.

There's a whole other level of social skills developing here that weren't previously available; so we've actually expanded in one direction as we've closed down in another. I saw awareness on his part, to navigate through this relationship, that I hadn't seen with him before. I wish he had that awareness in the rest of his world; that's the part we're working on. It's something he's not utilizing in other aspects of his life. I think the new social skills, shaped by the very access to technology, will provide some distinct advantages to live in this new world of technology.

One of the guidelines now, one of the "guy'isms" that gets mentioned from the confines of the couch in my office, is that you build the relationship on the phone and you break up, or you end the relationship, with text. It doesn't even have to be *"I'm breaking up with you."* Basically, what the teenage boys are telling me is that you just gradually shift from phone calls, to texts, then gradually spread them out until the conversation, as well as the relationship, fades away. It's a process by which the boy or girl can limit and change the level of intimacy over a period of time, and that's exactly what they want to do. It's a method of dealing with an uncomfortable social situation without really dealing with it. It just goes away. The teens tell me if you don't respond to text messages like, *"Why didn't you text me?"* or *"What are you doing?"* the deluge of messages will start to dwindle until they are over entirely. So the kids are actually playing with those dynamics and figuring them out. As a result, social rules, as they apply in a world of constantly changing technology, are completely being re-written.

Lisa and her husband sit on opposite sides of the family room playing Scrabble.

When Lisa's husband gets tired of losing, he yells at her, but no one hears a thing.

On the other side of the room their daughter is laughing.

Her cousin is also laughing.

They are texting each other.

So are Lisa and her husband.

He's not *really* yelling at her.

He's just telling her how stupid he thinks Scrabble is because she's beating him.

Lisa glances up at the clock and sends a text to their youngest child.

"It's time to go to bed" she says in the message and pushes 'Send.'

If this were an episode of the 1962 cartoon, *The Jetsons,* the only thing we might be missing in Lisa's family room is hearing George Jetson say, *"It's been light years since you programmed synthetic brownies."* The animated antics of George and his family were meant as a comical look into our future when all of the most modern conveniences would be at our fingertips. Well, here we are in a time when we can message each other instantly, all day long and into the night. So we talk less, but in some ways, we communicate more. It adds a flavor to our relationships we didn't have before the invention of Smart Phones. So there is a positive side, but learning the new rules of engagement will be required.

And that's what we're talking about when it comes to our children. There are new rules of engagement. Good or bad, it's a new battle. We are on a new battlefield. New technology, new ways to engage, and learning to parent the Facebook Nation is not unlike the changes our country's military must make. With the increase in technology, the rules of engagement have to change because now you have more control.

There have been instances in our nation's history when military teams didn't know who the insurgents were or exactly their location. It led to attacks on villages and the deaths of innocent people. But technology is so advanced, military strike squads have more information than ever about kill zones, and attacking an area of civilians because you didn't have the correct intelligence, is no longer an excusable offense.

As parents, trying to lead and guide this generation through the pitfalls, the land mines and the front lines of an unchartered battlefield, we have to be willing to subscribe to new rules of engagement. We have to use the same technology that has the potential to harm and use it for good. It may be their language, but wisdom often comes with age. As long as we are ready and willing to suit up, prepare for battle and make any adjustments necessary to stay on the cutting edge of change, we are half way home. Every aspect of what we are dealing with has a *"this but a that"* a *"good but also a bad"* a *"yes but sometimes a no"*. There is nothing definitive about a way of doing things that continues to evolve on a daily basis. We must evolve as parents and educators right along with the inventors who are introducing new technology into our world minute by minute. There is a saying that as a parent, *"I will say yes, until love demands that I say no."* We may need to subscribe to that theory, as part of our parenting arsenal, where our children's safety with technology is at stake.

We must also keep an open mind and see emerging technology, the World Wide Web, and the latest electronic gadgets as the miraculous inventions they are intended to be. I work with a young man who is currently in the third grade at one of the top private schools and he has Asperger's Syndrome. His struggle is writing.

I'm not talking about the creative process or the correct use of third grade grammar. It's the physical act of writing that is difficult for him. He can manage the hand strength, and his ability to write is good. He can print his letters and write in cursive. He can do all that, but physically putting pen to paper and coming up with concepts is very painful and difficult for him. The mountain he must climb is the blank piece of paper. He sees nothing. He doesn't know what to do with nothing. For him to create words from nothing is close to impossible. But when he looks at a computer keyboard, he sees words. To create words from letters that already exist, works very well for him. Technology is his saving grace.

One of the things his parents and the school have done to help him is to provide a new device known as the NEO 2. It's a lightweight portable word processor with a large keyboard and a screen that displays about two lines at a time. Compared with laptops and iPads, it's a very inexpensive device and holds several different files. It's the perfect tool for this young man and has literally changed his life. It has also improved the lives of his family and his teachers at school. He went from spending three to six hours every night doing homework that took most kids ten minutes to do, to now being able to do it in the same amount of time as his classmates.

It's an appropriate, beneficial and rewarding use of technology. He does have an iPad at home. But, while taking an iPad into the classroom for any third grader might not be a good idea, this young man, who is easily distracted, would probably end up playing games instead of using the device to further his education.   So, the use of the NEO 2, in a classroom setting, has turned out to be an amazing change for him. He's operating in the classroom environment better than he has ever been able to before.

The funny thing is that incorporating the device into the curriculum included a learning curve for all the adults.   We were trying to figure out how to download his work to another computer for printing, or better yet, how to plug his new device into a printer.   It took about 30 minutes and a specialist to come in and explain it to all of us.   This young man, in third grade, walked up and connected everything without anyone telling him how.   His mother was astonished.   We literally had seven people in the meeting, one of them was a technology specialist, and it took 30 minutes for everyone to understand how to download the information from this NEO 2 into a computer and print it.   The boy had a zero learning curve.   He walked up, grabbed it, plugged it in and printed it out.

This is a child who, before having access to this technology, literally had to be carried into the classroom because he hated school. He was afraid.   His fear of not knowing how to do something, not understanding the mechanics of writing, caused him to fear everything associated with learning.   As a result he didn't want to be there.

In the same vein, we can't allow any fear we might have of new technology to prevent us from utilizing everything available to us in our advancement of education.   Technology is here to stay.   We've passed the threshold and we see, as a society, what can be accomplished and what is possible. What we have to do now is compare and contrast the useful forms of technology with potentially harmful effects and find a workable balance between the two.

There used to be a rule of thumb among pediatric associations that children should be limited to about 90 minutes of *"television time"* in a given day, but due to the cultural changes our society is experiencing, the guidelines have been modified. The American Academy of Pediatrics now urges parents to limit *"screen time"* for one to two hours a day, keeping in mind that screen time incorporates far more than just the television set.

"Today's children are spending an average of seven hours a day on entertainment media, including televisions, computers, phones and other electronic devices. Media is everywhere. TV, Internet, computer and video games all vie for our children's attention. Studies have shown that excessive media use can lead to attention problems, school difficulties, sleep and eating disorders, and obesity. In addition, the Internet and cell phones can provide platforms for illicit and risky behaviors. The AAP recommends that parents establish "screen-free" zones at home by making sure there are no televisions, computers or video games in children's bedrooms, and by turning off the TV during dinner. Television and other entertainment media should be avoided for infants and children under age 2. A child's brain develops rapidly during these first years, and young children learn best by interacting with people, not screens."

A child's interaction

with others has always been a crucial part of early development. I suspect studies will eventually show a direct correlation between emotional and behavioral disabilities as well as a lack of social skills primarily the result of electronic surrogates. It's clearly just a matter of time. I'm already seeing evidence of it in my private practice.

So, even as we change the wording to say, *"screen time"* instead of *"television time,"* how do you define it? How do you quantify the quality of interactive time? From a research perspective, it's nearly impossible to compare a TV hour to an iPad hour, an iPhone, a Droid, a Blackberry hour compared to a Mac Air hour. How do you compare those hours of screen time? You can't do it. Yet qualitatively, I can tell you, there are certain applications and certain things we can do on computers that are actually beneficial. Engaged technology is something you can be actively involved with where you can learn skills that are beneficial later in life. Sure, you can watch an educational show on television but you're also being subjected to the commercials. There's a lot of down time and its passive learning instead of interactive learning. But how do you quantify that? How do you do the research and figure out how to measure it? And so unfortunately, from the organization with a goal for recommending to parents how much time is too much time, it's impossible. You can't accurately answer that question.

It's one of the problems we run into as we navigate these uncertain waters. There's not a good answer to how much "screen time" is safe. It's really up to parents, on an individual basis, to figure out what is best for each child. If you are trying to measure the impact precisely, you can't even have a hard and fast rule in your own family. Your daughter may be able to adapt to longer hours of technology time than your son, or vice versa. Two of your three children may not be as affected as the third child. And what about the amount of screen time that is required for their studies? How does that factor into the overall picture? How do parents limit time while also complying with the guidelines set forth in the classroom and for the allotted homework?

Parents will have to determine, in their own homes, what they consider to be engaged learning and what is not. What is the effect on their sleep? Some of the research already underway is looking at quantifiable effects on sleep patterns. We already know anything visual can cause hydro-stimulation in the brain. So then at what level and how much does technology interfere with sleep patterns? We can study it to the point of obtaining a minimum/maximum kind of guidepost. But, again, how do you quantify it? Does the amount differ if it's engaged learning? Does it differ if it's just visual stimulation? If so, are there other things in our environment that simultaneously over-stimulate visually? If so, what are those and how can they be defined and measured? It's complicated. I haven't seen anything that's addressing the issue. I've seen some articles on specific topics, like "sexting", or the impact of technology in a classroom, or the influence of technology on educational policies, but nothing that is really addressing the totality of the issue. The technological changes we have accepted into our lives, on face value, require us to do a total revamping of the way we raise children.

It's a plan we have to develop as we go, while being careful to police ourselves as the mentors and role models. Thus far, since we've already used the analogy of a ship out at sea, let me venture to say that, as adults, we're already letting a little water seep into the boat.

It had been just over a year since Gloria's husband died of leukemia.

She was home alone the day they would have celebrated their 50th wedding anniversary.

Her brother, sister-in-law and nephew came to cheer her up.

They had been there less than ten minutes when her brother and nephew pulled out their iPads.

The road trip had taken over two hours and they were anxious to check email and Facebook.

When Gloria's sister-in-law chastised them for their electronic distractions, her nephew started to put his away.

But when Gloria's brother continued surfing, so did her nephew.

Like father, like son.

Gloria said it was okay, even though everyone knew, it really wasn't.

Chapter 6

Who Needs Big Brother

When You Have A Volunteer Army?

Ft. Lauderdale looked like a sea of beach towels and bikinis.

The smell of sunscreen competed with the unmistakable aroma of cheap beer.

Jason and his friends were celebrating their fourth and final Spring Break.

They would graduate in May.

A booth set up with free tequila shots, for anyone over 21, quickly caught their attention.

The music was loud, the girls were pretty and no one could remember how many drinks they ended up ordering.

But when Jason passed out, his college classmate remembered to catch it all on his cell phone camera.

While everyone was still drunk, and thought it would be funny, Jason's friend posted the picture on Facebook.

"There was of course no way of knowing whether you were being watched at any given moment. How often, or on what system, the Thought Police plugged in on any individual wire was guess work. It was even conceivable that they watched everybody all the time. But at any rate they could plug in your wire whenever they wanted to. You had to live--did live, from habit that became instinct--in the

assumption that every sound you made was overheard, and, except in darkness, every movement scrutinized."

When Erick Arthur Blair, known more widely by his pen name, George Orwell, wrote those words, it was 1948. His haunting, yet fictional projections of a world in the year *1984*, depicted a society where every move, every word, every thought could be monitored. The idea that **BIG BROTHER IS WATCHING** became part of our pop culture. Over the next 35 years, readers took notice of Orwell's strange prophecies and according to a review in the *New York Times*, half feared they would come true the morning of January 1, 1984.

Now, here we are, almost as many years later, and lives are on display for all to see. But instead of being forced into submission by some totalitarian government, information is offered up on a volunteer basis. Register a new Wii gaming system and you will hand over permission for the creators in China to monitor your activity. Buy a new Apple iPhone and it comes complete with a tracking device. If you think Facebook is only viewable by "friends," you might need to check the Privacy Settings, which are subject to change. And how many people now drive with a GPS? If the device can locate where you are going, it already knows where you are.

Technology has twisted its way into our world so easily, so effortlessly that we have willingly gone along for the ride and relinquished many of our own rights to privacy. As parents, it is incumbent upon us to educate our children about mistakes they could possibly make from which we cannot rescue them.

Admissions personnel at many colleges and universities are already using Facebook as an investigative tool when processing paperwork for new applicants. Unless educated to navigate the possible pitfalls of a weekend beer bust, how are our children to know the life changing ramifications of one poor decision? We have to remember, we're dealing with teenage brains, hormones and peer pressure. Children sometimes do things they wouldn't normally do because of extenuating circumstances. We have to preempt the possible with information about the probable.

There are companies now requiring Facebook passwords to be included when filling out an application for employment. It sounds invasive. It sounds like a violation of your child's right to privacy. But does your child want the job once they've graduated? If so, many companies make it mandatory, viewing it no differently than a drug test.

In Jason's situation, a picture of him passed out on spring break, posted on Facebook, could easily keep him from getting his first job. Due to rising insurance premiums, many companies are no longer going to take the risk. Drinking to the point of passing out is dangerous behavior that might end up costing the company far more, in the long run, than the value of Jason as an employee. It's also something Jason's parents should have been aware of, warned him about and tried to protect him from before he ever left home.

Obviously, we can't control our children's behavior but we can educate them to make the wisest decisions possible.

As part of that education, we have to teach our children to be aware of each other. In Jason's situation, he wasn't the one putting the picture out there. But as we allow our children access to technology, we have to understand they are likely to test the boundaries. They're excited about the possibilities and challenged by their own peer groups to stay on top. As a result, some of them are taking technology to the next level. They're like immature private investigators. Back in the day, a spring break trip might produce a few tattle tales, some gossip about the inappropriate behavior of a few crazy kids; now, there's photographic evidence of your child's most vulnerable moments.

If you look back only one generation, being talked about behind your back at school, could be horrifying. It prompted more than one student to wake up sick the next day and not be able to attend classes. Now, our children are subject to being caught, not only on camera in compromising situations, but on video as well. There have even been cases where kids have purposely tried to catch other kids doing things they shouldn't, for the sole purpose of posting on Facebook. It's all fun and games until it's your son, who was photographed kissing another girl, when he's got a steady girlfriend, or when it's your daughter videotaped through the back window of a parked car. It's danger at a whole new level.

The depth of this danger was poignantly revealed in a

high profile case that came to light September 22, 2010. A young Rutgers University student jumped to his death from the George Washington Bridge in New Jersey after his roommate secretly videotaped him kissing another man. Dharun Javi not only watched what was happening with his roommate and another man behind closed doors, but also urged friends and Twitter followers to log into his web cam feed and view a second sexual encounter. Eighteen-year-old Tyler Clementi saw the Twitter posting and disabled Ravi's computer camera before taking his own life.

Ravi was arrested and charged with 15 crimes, in connection with the technological taunting, including intimidation and invasion of privacy. At his sentencing, he apologized, saying his actions were thoughtless, insensitive, immature, stupid and childish. But the damage was done. Two families were tragically broken. Ravi probably never even considered that his casual communication through social media could bring such heartbreaking circumstances.

On the day of the verdict, Clementi's mother released a statement saying, *"In this digital world, we need to teach our youngsters that their actions have consequences, that their words have real power to hurt or to help. They must be encouraged to choose to build people up and not tear them down."*

I know it's not always easy to talk to your children about sex or topics they might find embarrassing. It's even harder when they roll their eyes and assume they already know far more than you could ever tell them. But as parents, we should feel fortunate that our job of teaching them how to protect themselves, is far easier than theirs will be: learning to live in a world our ancestors couldn't begin to comprehend. For our children, it's not unlike being drafted to go off to war and walking forward with no idea where the land mines are located. There has to be some basic training if they are expected to survive.

Amanda knew from the get-go what she was doing.

It was the teenage boys, in her class at school, who were about to be fooled.

After what seemed like a little harmless flirting, Amanda asked for a few personal pictures via cell phone.

The boys sent them.

When one young man realized he was just being manipulated, he wanted his pictures back.

He asked, but that failed, so he tried to grab Amanda's cell phone in the hallway at school.

It didn't do any good.

She already had the pictures downloaded on her computer at home.

So he threatened to tell on her.

She got to the school office before he did.

Amanda portrayed herself as the victim who had received unsolicited pornographic images.

She had the pictures to prove it and the young man was expelled.

He was one of several boys who had fallen into Amanda's little trap.

And all those nude pictures were circulated among her circle of friends.

Amanda's situation is an example of an escalating problem that goes far beyond what we now know in our society as "sexting." In fact, we are currently counseling so many clients that, when they tell me they've come into a session because of "sexting", my reaction has almost reached the point of saying, *"So, it's just sexting? Oh thank goodness. It's just sexting."* I'm not trying to trivialize it, or minimize the magnitude of it, but the seriousness of children concocting their own recipes of sexuality, with the instant gratification provided through technology, is reaching entirely new levels.

When I was in school it was an urban myth that guys would wear mirrors on their shoes so they could look up a woman's dress. Now my daughters are in school and kids are taking pictures of other kids in the bathrooms without their knowledge. Girls are using cell phones to lure boys into a tangled web not unlike a prostitute on the seedy side of town. Boys and girls are using technology to publicize their own deepest secrets as well as those of other children without their permission. What started as erotic text messages, between boyfriends and girlfriends, just a few years ago, has morphed into pictures and videos with such sexually explicit material an X rating would be warranted. These are kids.

In Amanda's case, the first young man was flattered that she liked him. He was just a knuckle-headed hormonal young man looking to hook up with a new girl. It started innocently enough with her agreeing, by text, to go out with him. Then she messaged that it would be nice if he sent her some pictures of himself. He sent the teenage standard photos of his face and him standing in front of a mirror capturing, not only his image, but also that of the cell phone he was holding. It's a strange new photographic phenomenon in our children's online society.

Then Amanda quickly migrated to, " *Well that's not exactly what I meant.* " And the cryptic conversation continued, until the boy knew what she wanted, but anyone else reading her text messages might not get it.

As hard as it is for some parents to believe their fine young sons would do such a thing, it actually worked on several boys. Once they sent the pictures, her plan was in place to distribute, and they felt like she owned them. A foolish and spontaneous decision changed their lives. The price they've paid has been more severe than anything they expected, although, I doubt any of them really expected anything other than some quality time with a pretty girl.

When the first young man told his story, it sounded like an average shot at a weak defense, for the allegations against him. When other young men came forward, not even knowing about each other and telling the exact same story, the truth came out. But, the stories were told in confidence. So, Amanda remained the victim at school. At home, her parents weren't getting along and no one was checking her phone or computer. She was operating without fear. She was out there on the Internet without accountability. It's likely she still has those pictures stored on her computer.

Matthew came up with a new way to use the unlimited texting feature on his phone.

Girls outnumbered boys at his school three to one.

So getting a date was no problem.

What Matthew wanted to do was narrow it down.

.

He sent text messages to seven different girls.

As the conversations progressed he became more explicit with his language.

A couple of girls dropped out.

Then he started asking for pictures.

Another girl dropped out.

The four who were afraid not to give him what he requested, became the finalists.

But the one he asked out was the one who sent the most sexually suggestive photos.

It's not just about "sexting" anymore. In some instances it's moved on to intimidation, manipulation, power and control. Kids are using technology against other kids, when none of them really know the magnitude of what they are doing or how they are allowing themselves to be victimized. In order to guard and protect, we as parents, must venture into the controversial arena of a child's right to privacy.

I'm not adverse to the conversation that it's a violation of a child's rights to tap into their personal phone and computer accounts. But, then, I don't believe we currently live in a world where that's prudent. I don't think it's safe to let them go unchecked. If we can educate between the ages of three and eight, and if by the time they get to middle school, they've already heard it, they've learned it, and they have developed safe practices then maybe we can draw the line someplace in the future. I've always talked with parents about kids being allowed to have a diary. It's healthy for them to have a place where   they   get   to   be themselves without other eyes watching. They can share it with whom they choose or keep it to themselves. But even in those situations, I understand the parent who says *"Yes, but I think my child is doing drugs. And I think their diary is where I'm going to find the information."* The baseline I recommend is, **if it's a safety issue there are no privacy rules.**

It's the same policy we adhere to in our society and in our culture. We may not always agree with the government's ability to wiretap, or listen into conversations, or monitor certain things, but when it comes to terrorism and somebody trying to plan a strategy to blow up a building, we're not often opposed to the government checking it out. There are emergent safety issues with our children's use of technology, and I think we have to prioritize their wellbeing over their privacy.

It's a choice we make in our own home, and one that is not always black and white. As parents, we have to remain fluid in our approach to these sensitive issues and never hold ourselves to such a high standard that we are resistant to a continuing education of access. Our 14-year-old daughter knows we have the passwords to all of her accounts and we monitor them on a regular basis. As a matter of policy in our home, her cell phone, computer and iPad all get charged in our room overnight. I have parents that come into my office fearful after finding their child kept their cell phone in bed with them overnight. I will ask them if they checked the phone. They inevitably say no because they weren't sure if they should or not. When I suggest they ask their child about it, the answer usually comes back, *"Well, they said they were up until 3:00 in the morning talking."* Let's just say, as a matter of policy, in any home with school aged children, cell phone usage after bedtime is banned.

As I mentioned earlier though, it's not all black and white, yes or no, this way or that way. Sometimes we have to be flexible in our own parenting styles. Case in point.

One of the things I do is check our daughter's text messages, her emails and I run through her Facebook page to see what's going on. Where our family hit a snag was one night I grabbed her phone and checked it in front of her. At the time, we were all together watching a movie and her phone kept buzzing with incoming messages. I thought I was being funny when I snatched it up. She really got angry with me. Then the rest of the family threw their support behind her and all of a sudden I was the bad guy. It didn't change the fact that I still monitor her phone and her Internet activity, but I've conceded it's best to do it on my own time and not right in front of her. She knows I'm checking, but she doesn't have to sit and feel any embarrassment as her dad reads through her messages. I'm well aware, as I hope other parents are, that she can delete the messages she doesn't want me to see. So I try to check her phone at random times, maybe when she just gets up and leaves the room for a few minutes, and doesn't expect anyone to be looking. In those situations, I quickly check to see if any of the messages seem out of context, which might signal a series of messages that had been discarded. There are other parents who adhere to the policy that the cell phone must be handed over on demand. If the child resists, then phone privileges are temporarily lost. It prevents them from erasing the last few messages and gives a more accurate gauge of what is happening at the moment. They are motivated to cooperate by the dreaded teenage fear of losing their phone.

In general I think our daughter is a pretty mature typical teenager. I don't think she's out doing a bunch of nefarious actions that would necessitate her hiding anything. If she did delete texts, I suspect it would be because she's trying to date some new boy and doesn't want me to know yet. I don't believe we are at the point of "sexting" or any other dangerous behavior. But we could be. And that's one of the reasons I do spot checks. I'm not naïve. I know it can happen.

Lainey and her friend Lilly were goofing around like teenage girls sometimes do.

They were both dressed in pajama pants and spaghetti strap t-shirts taking funny posed pictures.

Since the girls were in the privacy of their own bedrooms, they uploaded the photos for each to see.

They put them on Facebook, but only in an album meant for the eyes of the other.

The photos were artsy and cool but their bedroom attire accentuated their maturing bodies.

Lainey only intended Lilly to see the pictures and Lilly went forward with the same plan.

What the girls didn't think about, was all their Facbeook friends, boys and girls, could see them.

All they had to do was click on "Photos" and there they were.

Their bedrooms and their pajamas were no longer private.

Big Brother may not be watching, but a lot of other people are. Lainey is my 14-year-old daughter. So as not to embarrass her again, I publish this story only with her permission. In a home with a Watchdog Dad like me, even the smallest, innocent acts can easily become risky behavior when put in a place where privacy is lost, even accidentally. She wasn't thinking that someone else could go in and look at the pictures, even save them to their own computers and re-publish them elsewhere. This was just supposed to be between her and her friend Lilly. But wearing your pajamas in front of your best friend, is way different than wearing your pajamas for the whole world to see.

We may not be as technologically savvy as our children, but hopefully we are all more mature. There is no time in the foreseeable future when we can let our guards down and let them go it alone. They need our guidance. They need to be educated. They need us to stand up for them on the frontlines of these potential mine fields and help them assess what may be hidden. As a good driver's eyes dart back and forth, from side to side, always looking for anything that might possibly cause an accident, we must constantly survey these new social networks. No one is forcing us to hand our children over to a totalitarian society like the one Orwell wrote about in *1984*. We **are** willingly allowing access to dangerous tools when we're not yet sure of our own boundaries. Many parents, especially those in the Baby Boomer generation want to be friends with their children. It makes it harder to hold the line where discipline and decisive parenting are concerned. We live in a time when the focus has drifted away from the family and the spotlights have been trained on the children. It may be difficult to ask your teenage son for help setting up your new iPad and then restricting his use of the laptop an hour later. But parenting has never been easy. It takes persistence, perseverance and an iron will. In the words of Abraham Lincoln, *"You cannot escape the responsibility of tomorrow by evading it today."* We can't afford to wait until our children have made irreparable mistakes before we intervene. When you put this book down, go find out what your kids are doing on their laptop, watching on their iPad, saying on their cell phone. Check their video files and their picture files. You may find yourself surprised. Hopefully relieved. But you won't know for sure until you take that brave step and place your child's safety over their comfort or your discomfort. **If it's a safety issue there are no privacy rules!**

Leann wanted her friend to go on the family vacation.

The friend was invited, but when there were scheduling conflicts, she had to decline.

Leann had just turned 18 and wanted some freedom from her parents to meet new friends.

She had been more obedient than usual and so they let her go off on her own.

They were a little uncomfortable about the crowd she chose, but they didn't want to ruin her vacation.

Several weeks after returning home, Leann's mother received a phone call.

It was the mother of the friend who had not been able to come along.

She was highly critical of the provocative pictures she had seen of Leann on Facebook.

The pictures, of Leann and several young men, had been taken on the vacation.

They were pictures her parents had never seen.

They were pictures her parents never knew existed.

The photos alone told a story of a vacation much different than the one her family had experienced.

The pictures alerted them to a girl adrift on a sea of trouble.

Making the high school drill team should have been one of the most exciting times in Elaine's life.

She was a rising 9th grader and had been chosen to represent her high school in the flag corps. But she was caught off guard when she showed up for practice and one of the older girls was glaring at her. The girl took it a step further and started talking about Elaine to a group of other girls. Although Elaine knew some of girls on the team, she didn't know the mean girl.

Then it clicked. The night before she had received several Facebook "Friend Requests". She accepted those she knew and ignored those she didn't. The girl staring at her must have been one of the ones she had set aside. Elaine didn't want someone she hadn't even met having access to her Facebook page. But now she felt pressured to accept the request in order to avoid the drama.

Chapter 7

Ain't It Good To Know You've Got A Friend?

In 1971, Carole King wrote it out clearly and James Taylor made the words famous. *"When you're down and troubled and you need a helping hand and nothing, whoa, nothing is going right. Close your eyes and think of me and soon I will be there to brighten up even your darkest nights."* A friend, we all knew, was someone you could call on, someone you could count on, and someone who would be there for you no matter what. *"You just call out my name, and you know wherever I am, I'll come running to see you again. Winter, spring, summer or fall, all you have to do is call and I'll be there, yeah, yeah, you've got a friend."*

Friends were divided up into easily understandable categories. We had school friends, work friends, family friends, and casual friends, close friends and sometimes a best friend. But now, we have hundreds of friends. And the question is worthy of asking, has Facebook friendship changed the definition of "friend"? I think that's a whole new concept. And so what does that mean? What is the implication of that from the standpoint of future relationships? Does that water down the concept of what friendship really is? Does it even matter anymore; or, is everybody going to be a friend? Even if you don't like them, or you don't really know them, do you still accept their "Friend Request"? How do we distinguish between who is really a friend and who is not a friend? And if we're going to agree to be friends with people who aren't really friends, why are we doing this? What does that open us up to? And does that then water down the communication we have with people who are actually friends that we see face to face? If we know we have friends that aren't really friends, then do we censor the things we say, or say everything we want to say, and face the consequences? How does that impact my interpersonal non-technology based relationships? Does it really change how we view friendships as a whole?

It sounds a little convoluted. I want it to sound that way, because it is.

Elaine's first instinct was to correct her mistake.

If she had hurt someone's feelings by not "friending" them on Facebook, then she would just accept the request.

But Elaine's parents cautioned her to reconsider.

If the girl became angry, glared at her and tried to isolate her from the group, was that really a friend?

Since Elaine didn't know who the girl was at first, but now knew, she thought it would be okay."We're friends with lots of people on Facebook," she told her parents.

"That's just part of it. It's just your friends."

It used to be, when we found out someone was upset with us, we would wonder if we had said something that might have been repeated. Now, it seems it's almost automatic to assume or at least question it would be, if you have offended someone online. I find it interesting that we're in a sociological place where one of the first and most direct thought processes, especially among children who are using technology as their primary form of communication, is whether a slight was cyber-sourced.

The Merriam-Webster Dictionary says the word, "friend" originated before the 12th century in Old English with *frēon,* to love, and *frēo,* which means free. Friend is defined as *"one attached to another by affection or esteem."* So, just as a little experiment, I checked to see how I fare among three randomly selected Facebook friends. I was among 688 friends on one page. I was listed as a friend with 1,069 other friends on another page. And finally, in a shining example showing just how significant an online relationship can be, I was one of 2,210 friends listed on another page. I am an adult, well trained in the science of human psychology. And I have to wonder if the definition of "friend" should include "someone you *really* know. "

But how much more basic can it get? Do I say "yes" or "no" to a Friend Request? Then how completely complicated can it be when you consider all the ramifications of what can actually happen now and later? If Elaine opens up her page to a girl she doesn't really know, that girl will have access to Elaine's pictures, comments, important dates, the things she likes and all her other friends. Possibly more alarming, after demonstrating her anger toward Elaine, the girl would have the ability to post anything she wanted to say on Elaine's page. It gets even more risky when you recognize that it's even harder to undo what has been done. If Elaine says "yes" and then later decides "no, "the process of "un-friending" someone can be more of a slam to them than never accepting the person's request in the first place. It's a whole new layer of interpersonal dynamics that we didn't have before technology took over a big part of what used to be our private lives.

As a doctor and as a parent, I see the pitfalls our children are facing as they begin to develop different personalities, based on the tangibility of friends they can touch, and associations they align themselves with over the Internet. There's even a new element of interpersonal injuries that can occur through technology that some people haven't yet realized. There was a time when a teenager might stress over a birthday party guest list for fear of accidentally forgetting a friend or upsetting someone who was purposely not invited because they didn't know them well enough. Now it's not even an actual event. It's a cyber community where you have to be confirmed in order to get in. But you don't necessarily have to be a "friend" to get flagged with a "Friend Request". Some requests are tossed out solely based on the fact that you are friends with a friend of the one who wants to be your friend. Other requests are based on the commonality of where you work, or where you go to school, or by someone you met on a recent vacation that you would probably never see again. Do you say *"yes?"* Or, do you say, *"I don't really know this person"* and let the request go unaccepted? This generation's peer pressure prompts kids to go ahead and say *"yes"* so they can have as many friends as possible. But then what does that open them up to versus being selective? And then, how does their list of friends begin to shape their online identity against who they are in person?

Do we educate children on how to have two different personas? Do we teach them to have an on-line persona and, if so, what does that look like? Then do we teach them how to have an in-person interpersonal persona, and what does that look like?

Madison had never taken the time to set up a Facebook account.

It wasn't really something she was all that interested in doing.

But then a friend died suddenly, and it seemed all lines of communication ran through the online community. At the funeral, prodded by all the kids who once hung out together, she agreed to set up a page.

She had to admit it was fun responding to the friend requests and catching up with people from her past.

But then a week later, Madison made a mistake.

Someone posted a political opinion and Madison responded with hers. All of a sudden her new Facebook page was inundated with insults. It left her feeling embarrassed and exposed.

But it taught her a valuable lesson about the person she could, and could not be, on Facebook.

We've probably all had friendships based on something superficial. Career climbers are not strangers to shaking the correct hands and networking with successful sources. As children, we learn quickly who has a pool or a pony. In high school, the kid with the first car is about as popular as the captain of the football team or the head cheerleader. And in college, often times those with the means to finance the best parties are the ones you will find with all the friends.

Liev Schreiber, a Hollywood actor who has been cast in many diverse roles, understands the concept through the lens of fame.

"There's the private persona and the public persona and the two shall never meet." Similarly, there is an online persona and an in-person persona. Let's face it; many of those frequenting online dating sites perfected this concept years ago.

As a young lady just beginning to get her feet wet in the turbulent waters of social networking, should Madison's parents advise her to set aside her own opinions and keep silent? Or should they tell her to act one way on Facebook, and another way with close friends she actually sees on a regular basis? Or, would it be best, now that she knows the impact her opinions can have on her online group of friends, to be who she really is, come what may? If we develop different personas ourselves, or educate our children in the art of what some might suggest is deception, then how do we manage it and how do we teach them to manage it?

In one sense, it might seem as sinister as the fictional DC Comics character, Two-Face. The archenemy of Batman was once Harvey Dent, the clean-cut district attorney of Gotham City. But after being severely scarred and taking on his "Two-Face" persona, Dent flips a coin to decide if he should bring about good or evil.

On the other hand, it can be as simple as calculating the type of image you might want to project in order to put your best foot forward. Daniel J. Boorstin, professor, historian, writer and the 12th Librarian of the United States Congress, knew how important it was to make a good appearance. *"An image is not simply a trademark, a design, a slogan or an easily remembered picture. It is a studiously crafted personality profile of an individual, institution, corporation, product or service."*

This is probably the first generation that has been encouraged to have a continuously growing list of ways in which they've served. Volunteer hours as well as extra-curricular activities have become important elements of university and college entrance applications. *"It will look good on your resume,"* has been a catch phrase kids have heard over the years as they have grown up and begun eyeing possible career opportunities. You can even hire people to perfect your resume to cast a certain impression and set yourself apart from all the others jockeying for the job. But we've added an element, a layer of how we are portrayed, by setting up profiles on social networking sites. And with the concept of "Timelines," it's not even just how our personal profiles or our children's profiles look today, but how we've allowed ourselves to be seen all along. Schools, colleges, universities and prospective employers can now go back and look at how our lives have played out online for years. Will they see who we really are or only what we wanted them to see? It's a situation that has to be addressed. Educators and parents who continue to delay the discussion are only gambling with results that may not be repairable. We have to educate early and often. We have to move forward, knowing there are different personas. It's complicated. It's complicated for adults, much less kids, to try and figure out those dynamics and the impact they can have in the short term and certainly in the long run.

We've never seen anything like this before. We've not experienced anything this social or this broad in scope. We've jumped on board aware and, in some cases, unaware of all the privacy concerns and all the other issues that come with it. But it's enticing.

And, there is a good side that includes a legitimate positive avenue of human interaction that allows for the ability to manage and maintain relationships beyond what we had the capacity for previously. How many billions of dollars have been raised for charities? How much marketing has been available for businesses? How many organ donors have saved lives that might once have been lost? How many long lost loves have been rekindled? How many adopted children have found their birth parents? It is a tool that can be used for evil or good. But, unlike "Two-Face", we cannot leave it to the toss of a coin. We go back to the beginning and the wise words of Spiderman, *"With great power comes great responsibility."* It's a struggle, a balancing act and a risk. But in it there is great reward if we educate and act responsibly.

Caleb lives in an online gaming forum.

It's his world. His friends are spread out all over the country and every night they chat. It's been his primary means of communication for several years and now Caleb is 17.

But this year, when two girls in the forum began to fight for his attention, Caleb was asked to leave.

The forum moderator has ultimate power and felt that Caleb was at fault.

Being kicked out, even for a day, was the single worst thing that could have happened to Caleb. He wasn't just excluded from one or two friends; his entire world was taken away.

When Caleb's grandparents first brought him to see me, they didn't believe he had any friends. They were confused and justifiably concerned. What I tried to help them understand is that Caleb has a lot of friends. They are just all online. He has already accepted, recognized and adopted a new definition of friend. Caleb believes friendship is a positive, long-term relationship that can be defined in broad terms to include Internet connections he's never actually met. He's had years of relationships with these friends through text, chat and the gaming forum.

But it still didn't seem that simple to the grandparents who are raising Caleb. In their minds, friends are people you hang out with.

Caleb doesn't hang out with anybody; it's just not what he does. It's not what he enjoys. It's not something he's probably ever going to do.

He's just not somebody who likes to hang out. His grandparents define friends differently than he does. Their context of friendship comes from their generation and that of Caleb's parents. But things have changed. Technology has changed us. And I would have to say Caleb has friends. His cyber friends affect him, his moods and attitudes are altered as a result of being in community with them, and even though he doesn't "know" them in person, he knows about them. He understands them. He may never take those relationships to an in-person level, but isn't that still a relationship? Has the definition of friend been changed by technology? It's not necessarily good or bad.

But it's definitely different. I think there's a generational difference that we have to recognize and be willing to accept in order to accommodate a new definition.

Unfortunately, what I frequently find when talking with parents, or in Caleb's situation his grandparents, is that many of them think the children will eventually come to realize this cyber world isn't real. They believe the kids will come to their senses and recognize real relationships are of the tangible type. But I also work with clients who are already adults, and all their friendships are being maintained through Facebook, chat rooms, forums, Instant Messaging and text. They live in different states or different countries and it doesn't matter to them.

They don't feel the need for a friend who will come running to help them change a flat tire, move into a new apartment or meet them at the local pub. They feel fulfilled with their online relationships.

This new normal is permeating our society at all levels. The Disney Channel's sitcom *Good Luck Charlie* is just one recent example of how common it's becoming. Charlie's older sister Teddy and her BFF Ivy share one of those priceless teenage girl moments.

Ivy: Are you ready for the big news?
Teddy: Yeah always
Ivy: Here goes…there's a guy.

Teddy: There's a guy? Who is he?

Ivy: He's that new guy in our government class, Raymond.

Teddy: Oh he's cute. When did you start talking to him?

Ivy: Well we haven't actually talked yet. We've been IM'ing that led to texting now he wants to step it all the way up to video chat. I don't know if I'm ready.

It's intended to make us laugh at what might have seemed like an absurdity just a few years ago. But it is our current reality. And as educators, parents, doctors, authority figures, we've got to open our minds and hearts to all that is changing around us, and just as important, we've got to keep pace.

In the immortal words of the great philosopher Mark Twain, *"When I was a boy of fourteen, my father was so ignorant I could hardly stand to have the old man around. But when I got to be twenty-one, I was astonished by how much he'd learned in seven years. "* The truth for us was our parents did know more than we did, we just didn't think they did. But now there are areas in the educational process, especially in the field of technology, where some children and many teenagers actually do know more than their parents. If an adolescent has real evidence that their parents don't understand what they are talking about, it's different than them just saying, *"You don't understand me."* It creates a very difficult and sometimes painful divide. As I see it, parents still have wisdom, knowledge and understanding of the major issues their children will face as they mature. But finding a way to maintain the child's respect while disseminating that information becomes an ongoing process.

When we age, we get further away from a younger population and it takes more and more work to stay relevant to that population. As a doctor, I have to stay abreast of the main changes in technology in order to stay relevant. I must be able to communicate with my teenage clients, who make up the majority of my clients, in order to help them.

It is also necessary for me to keep up as I parent a teenage daughter and try to comprehend continuously changing technology before my four-year-old reaches her adolescent years. With clients, or my own kids, I have to keep their attention spans. I have to be able to talk in relevant ways. I have to be able to connect with the clients that I'm working with or I can't build the level of trust needed in order to have a good therapeutic relationship. I have to be able to communicate with my own children or risk losing their respect.

Right now, in my profession, there are very few guidelines for what we do, and how or why we do it when it comes to factoring in technology. But I can easily say technology is already changing how we do things and the way we interact. The guidelines, even as more are written, are always going to have to be in flux. The clients are different. The teenagers are different. We can't hold conversations in the same way we did ten or 20 years ago. The attention spans and the topics have changed.

I'm an early adapter in technology. I think that's what enables me to remain relevant with adolescents. I understand their world at some level. I don't understand it at the same level that they do, but I know enough about their world that I can still hold a conversation with them and they don't completely write me off.

As a parent, I urge you to stay the course as we map our way through the uneven terrain of all this new technology.

We are all in this together.

Ain't it good to know you've got a friend?

As soon as they saw me, Lainey and Taylor's eyes were drawn to the cut on my lip.

"Daddy, what happened?" Taylor asked.

"Yeah, Dad," Lainey joined in. "You've got a cut on your lip. What did you do?"

"Well, girls," I told them. "I was reading in bed and my iPad slipped out of my hand and bopped me in the lip."

The girls giggled.

But here was one of those priceless teachable moments.

You have to be careful.

Technology can hurt you.

And it can even change the way you look! ☺

A big screen television, the Christmas tree and all the presents made for a pretty nice photograph.

There was a little girl, all snuggled up in her parent's bed, surrounded by stuffed animals.

A picture of the same child

eating a Popsicle in the kitchen depicted all the items kept on the counter top.

The backyard pool, front porch swing and trampoline could be seen somewhere in the photo albums.

You could even look into the teenage boy's bedroom, after his mom snapped a picture of him playing guitar.

There were photos taken at work, at school and of course on all the family vacations.

Almost anything you might want to know about these people was there in digital color.

Of course, the albums were only available to a few hundred of their closest friends on Facebook.

Chapter 8

It doesn't matter who is on the outside;

We'll let almost anyone look in

Storyteller, author and scholar of psychology, Michael Meade, says it like this, *"A false sense of security is the only kind there is."* And yet, Forbes.com, in an annual survey of how the wealthiest 20 percent of Americans spend their money, reports a 157% increase in purchases of home security systems.   **ADT** advertises they are *"Always There."*   **Protect America** warns us, *"Don't Be Out of Touch."*   And **Xfinity** persuades, *"Protect Your Home and Family for Total Peace of Mind."*   But none of these security systems are set up to notify us when we voluntarily open our own doors via the Internet.

Long before any of us were online, a series of television vignettes called *Friends of the Family* portrayed a professional wrestler, a gangster, a Rambo-type figure and a roller derby queen shoving their way past a mother and into a family home to hang out and watch television with a young boy. The message at the time revolved around televised violence: ***"Do You Know Who Your Children Are Inviting Into Your Home?"***   We've come a long way since then, and have become so accustomed to social sharing, that just about every aspect of our lives is out there entrusted in the hands of a lot of people, some we barely know.

Lea's grandfather was in the public eye.

He was had accomplished notoriety from many direction.

When Lea's mother was just 12-years-old, an obsessed "friend" tried to kidnap her.

He had been using binoculars to watch the family home from a nearby rooftop.

The man had a job with a local construction crew and easily disguised himself as a roofer.

Years later, the same stalker came looking again.

This time, he attempted to breech the family's security through Lea's online social networking sites.

Apparently, the man thought if he could contact Lea through her Facebook page, he could get to her mother.

Lea grew up being educated on the dangers associated with fame.

She was told many times to be cautious with the personal and family information she shared.

And because Lea's parents were diligent and continuously monitored her online activity, no one was harmed.

Unfortunately, the story doesn't always end as well as Lea's. In October 2009, a 33-year-old man living in his car found a way to "friend" a 17-year-old college student on Facebook. The man used a fake profile to present himself as a teenage boy. When the young girl agreed to a first meeting, she was kidnapped, raped and murdered.

Monitoring our children's online activity has never been more necessary. In doing so, we must recognize, as hard as we are trying to stay one step ahead, there are others attempting to lure our children into a pit of secrecy, where even the most vile images and websites can be concealed. The website WikiHow tells children and teens, in just eight simple steps, how to surf the Internet without their parents knowing. But Wiki.Answers.com takes it to another level, giving detailed instructions on how to hide pornography from parents.

There was a time, not so long ago, when teenage boys hid their Playboy magazines under their mattress, in the dark corner of a closet or behind a bookcase. Wherever they chose to hide it, whether they got away with it or not, it was still there. There was physical evidence parents could lay hold of and prove what their son was doing behind their backs. Now, as parents, we can be looking, and still miss it. There are numerous options if a child chooses to be deceptive. And, quite frankly, they don't even have to try all that hard. Most browsers, whether Chrome, Safari or Explorer have privacy settings where you can surf without being tracked…or you can track your history, yet go in and choose what part of it you want to delete.

Christian's mother had heard about parents finding electronic devices in their children' beds.

But she thought she knew her son well enough not to worry about such things.

One morning, quite innocently, she was looking for his ipad in order to use it herself.

She searched his room, the living room, kitchen and den but couldn't find it.

Finally, when Christian woke up, she found it in his bed.

When she checked the history, it was blank.

Fearing that overreacting might create a divide between them, she sat him down for a calm discussion.

She told him she already knew he was trying to hide something; it was just a question of what it might be.

They sat at the kitchen table for a good long while before he finally admitted to looking at pornographic pictures.

As I continuously advise my clients, Christian's mother used the situation to educate him on the dangers of what he was doing, rather than taking it as an opportunity to punish him. Adolescent boys and girls are curious. We were, when we were growing up, and they are no different. They just have a far different level of access to all that is out there, than we ever did. So, what do we do? We do the only thing we can do. We educate them. We prepare them. If you read this entire book and you walk away with only one message, I hope it will be to educate early and often. Parents, teachers and school administrators must be willing to have open and honest conversations. We need to be communicating about what they are going to see in the event they find their way to one of these websites. We have to help remove the *"OMG"* factor. In some cases, things that are forbidden become that much more enticing to the person who is being told not to do it or not to look at it. So we take away the *"WOW"* factor, the *"This is so cool"* part of looking at something they shouldn't, and through education, we teach them to have a more mature response such as, *"Oh yeah I've heard about that. We've really got to be careful here. This is not a place we probably need to go."*

Smoking is a perfect example. Smoking rates have drastically decreased and it's not just one factor, its multiple factors. But the primary reason kids are smoking less now than in years past is education. The tipping point of education has been that smoking really isn't cool. Kids have been taught to be more health conscious and they've seen the gruesome reality of people battling lung cancer. There is certainly a segment where it's still believed to be cool. And kids are going to try things. They are especially going to try things that they perceive are cool, that their friends say are cool. But some of them will take the opposite position, going counter to what everybody else is doing. They will maintain that doing something that is not cool is cool because it's cool to be not cool. Kids are just going to try stuff. They are going to experiment and get their own answers instead of always listening to the adults around them who have probably already tried it themselves. Kids are going to explore. But what eventually happens is when the majority of the messages are consistent, and the majority of the cool kids begin to say no, because they've been educated and are making an educated choice, then education wins the battle. You do find pockets of resistance in various socioeconomic circles and areas where rebellion has more to do with smoking than the actual desire to smoke.

Brittany has a job making $7.25 an hour.
When she gets her paycheck, she has to pay her car insurance and buy gasoline.
The pack of cigarettes she was smoking cost $5.56.

At the height of her habit, the 16-year-old Brittany was smoking a pack a day.

After a few lessons on budgeting and finance, she was able to figure it out for herself.

She could work almost an hour in order to pay for her pack of cigarettes.

Or, she could work that same amount of time, put more gas in her car and go hang out with her friends.

What she learned made more sense to her than the smoking.

All she did was make a rational decision based on information.

Learning lasts a lifetime if we want to live our lives to the fullest. If we want to give our children the best chance to succeed, then we have to educate early and often. Smoking stinks, it's expensive, and it causes cancer. We really haven't had any trouble relaying that message to the masses. But when it comes to talking about sex in our society, we still don't like to do it in front of the kids.

"Everyone knows that the Internet is changing our lives, mostly because someone in the media has uttered that exact phrase every single day since 1993. However, it certainly appears that the main thing the Internet has accomplished is the normalization of amateur pornography. There is no justification for the amount of naked people on the World Wide Web, many of whom are (clearly!) doing so for non-monetary reasons." It's a funny quote from the author of **Sex, Drugs and Cocoa Puffs**, Chuck Klosterman, but it's a serious situation. Pornography is as accessible to kids now as a 35

cent pack of cigarettes was back in 1960. Even worse, Internet pornography can come right into their rooms for free.

In order to prepare our kids for what may confront them, we have to find ways of opening up the lines of communication. We need to have conversations, learn how to articulate our arguments and stand strong against our own embarrassing insecurities for the sake of our children. They need this information.

In Christian's case, he knew what he was doing didn't feel right. The secrecy alone made him feel guilty. But looking at the online images of naked women had a payoff. As much as he told himself to stop doing it, the opportunity would present itself again and he would look again.

I don't have all the answers as a dad or a doctor, but I believe most of our kids want to have healthy relationships as they grow up. Many of them want to marry and have families. It's incumbent upon us to help them understand that allowing the outside evils of pornography into their lives through the Internet will have a negative impact on their future relationships. It may be a message we have to experiment with a few times before we get it right and get them to believe what we're saying, but I believe it can be done. We did it with smoking.

Teenagers are already being cautioned about the dangers of sexually transmitted diseases and unwanted pregnancies. But many of them may not know that continuous viewing of online pornography can actually alter the level of stimulation their bodies will need to become sexually satisfied. If you're training your brain to recognize that the pornography you are seeing is what's stimulating, that it's what is exciting, it becomes very difficult to have a healthy mutual relationship or sexual relationship later in life.

You don't have to look far to see a segment of our society where kids are being left unattended and unsupervised on the Internet. It's in their adolescent nature to want to be the one who has the salacious information, the one who has seen it, the one who has done it. The "cool" factor comes into play and then there is peer pressure to check it out, sneak a peek, see what it is all about. Again, the curiosity is no different than it was when girlie magazines were passed around a boy's locker room. But what they are seeing, what they are experiencing, what they may never be able to forget, is very different!

Maybe you are a parent who doesn't believe your child would ever look at online pornography. It's easy to develop a false sense of security when you feel like you really know your child. But just as Christian's mother was caught off guard by something she thought her son would never do, we can't buy into the idea that it's alright for our children to be using all these electronic devices in the privacy of their own rooms. We need to be around when they are surfing. They need to be somewhere they can be monitored at all times. None of us would hand our child a loaded gun and tell them it was okay to go into their bedroom and lock the door. Parents who allow their children unlimited Internet access with absolutely no supervision are asking for lethal results.

Chris's mother thought she had the simplest of solutions.

Since her son had already been in some trouble, she decided he wouldn't be able to have a Facebook page.

Chris was 15 and about to start a new school.

Facebook wasn't his first priority, but his friends sort of assumed he would have one sooner or later.

The biggest problem for all those on the outside looking in was that Chris' mom had a Facebook page.

Of course they also knew if Chris really wanted one, his mom probably couldn't stop him.

You can't create a fortress. There's no digital fortress in today's world. Chris will probably just go to school and have a Facebook page at school. Or he will find a friend who welcomes his use of their computer. If a kid wants a Facebook page bad enough or if they want to get online and have been forbidden to do so, they will most likely find a way. But here is the problem Chris's mom may not be anticipating. It creates a greater divide between she and her son. First, he sees her as being a bit of a hypocrite. She has a Facebook page, yet she forbids him to have one. Then, if he goes against her rule, his disobedience creates an even greater divide in their relationship. It creates a distance in the family that is extremely dangerous. If Chris chooses to go online in secrecy, then he begins living a whole life his parents know nothing about.

There are going to be parents who say you can't do this, you can't have this, and maybe the kids will be compliant. But we're at a point where it's very hard not to let them live in the digital world. And if you're not going to allow them at least some access to the world around them, then you have to face the fact that there are going to be some serious consequences. Every day I am seeing situations like this one where parents and children are at odds over online activity and they need a third party to mediate.

A June 2012 article in AARP magazine listed a number of fixtures in our every lives that will, sooner rather than later, be obsolete because of all the emerging technology. Among those listed are answering machines, analog clocks *("Our cell phones synch perfectly to satellites never forget to spring forward")* house phones, desktops, film, road maps and the list goes on. As movie rental stores, bookstores and snail mail move away from our landscape, those of us in the therapy profession only see our business growing. People don't change. You can add all the technology in the world, but people still need a way to deal with the complexity of the situation. And so that's ultimately the world of psychology, therapy and counseling. Our profession helps people deal with stress. Our lives are not less stressful with technology, they're actually more stressful, more complicated with more, rather than less, dynamics and I see no letup in sight.

So what I do is work with families on trying to make healthy, rational decisions, while accepting the totality of the family environment. If a parent or a family comes in, I'm not going to say, *"No, you've got to let your kids have a Facebook page!"* I'm going to say, *"Okay, let's look at how we are actually going to make this happen. What are the consequences? How is it going to affect you? And how are you willing to live with those consequences? How are you going to handle it?"* I stand in the gap and try to help the family find a proper balance as we look for solutions that will work to minimize their division. I try to help parents understand that they can't agree that we live in a digital culture while simultaneously forbidding their children to be a part of it. It doesn't work that way. A hard line like that only creates anger, frustration and a need for secrecy among the children.

Although we are trying to navigate some unchartered waters with all the new technology, the deliberation over allowing or not allowing children to have access is not unlike the decision parents and children have been making for decades about dating. The standard age many families feel is appropriate for dating is age 16. So let's say everyone in the family agrees. The teenager and both parents are all on board. Will everyone stick by that determination? How will they adhere to it? What happens when *"everyone else at school"* begins dating at 14 or 15? How will you stand your ground in your own family? How do you deal with it? How, as a parent, will you prepare your child for the disappointment or frustration along the way? Will you manage it? How do you keep it from being a divisive issue within the family? If everyone agrees on 16, but then it appears everyone else's family has decided on 14, it's going to cause problems. Kids want to do what other kids are doing. Parents have to be parents, and our decisions are not always popular. But just like debating the proper age for dating, we now have to make decisions about being on Facebook, surfing the Internet behind closed doors, talking by texting so no one in the room knows what is being said, and choosing a set of friends from a chat room. You can mandate that your children are not going to be allowed to do these things, but as with other such decisions, you have to prepare for and recognize there are going to be ramifications if the agreements are broken. There are going to be consequences. There is going to be pushback. What you have to decide is how you are going to handle it? How are you going to deal with it so that it conforms to what is best for the entire family?

Just as there are segments of our society that will continue to smoke no matter the cancer statistics, warnings, or amount of educational material, there are also parents who will believe their kids are no more in jeopardy in 2012 than they were back in 1976. Baby Boomers tried things. Baby Boomers were curious. As parents, and even educators, many have tried smoking, drinking, drugs and an occasional glance at a pornographic video. So there will be those among us who think it's okay. The kids will experiment and then they'll move on. But the stakes are higher. The price they may have to pay is greater. And they deserve to have all the information we can provide them so that they can then make an educated decision about the things they will do that may alter the course of their entire lives.

Our society is so sexualized, yet no one seems comfortable talking about it. Sex sells, and we see it displayed on billboards, television, bookshelves and department store windows. Because we've yet to bring it out into the light for a cultured conversation, it remains shrouded in darkness and secrecy. It leaves us all feeling worse, not better. We've got to act like adults and accept we are not our parents and this is not the same world in which they lived. We've got to remove the shroud of secrecy, educate our children so they know what is out there before they get caught up in it or before they fall victim to someone who sees them as easy prey. Our children have a right to know that the pornography they sneak a peek at under the covers of their bed can be just as addictive as any cigarettes they will ever smoke. They need to know what to do *before* a sexual predator tries to "friend" them on a social networking site. *"It's hard to come up with an example of a sexual predator who doesn't use some form of social networking anymore," according to Steve DeBrota, an assistant U.S. attorney in Indianapolis who prosecutes child sex crimes*

We've been teaching our young children about "stranger danger" for years. The difference now is that the boogieman can come into our homes electronically, if no one is watching.

A 42-year-old Monterey, Tennessee man was lucky he ended up with nothing more than a bloody nose.

After making contact with a 12-year-old girl on Facebook, the man attempted to lure her out of her home.

The girl's father, diligently monitoring the Facebook messages, set up his own sting operation.

When the alleged would-be predator showed up at the designated meeting place, the dad called police.

But before police arrived, the girl's dad punched the man.

The man claimed he just wanted to befriend the girl and told police he deserved to be punched.

Chapter 9

Putting the Text in Context

k

Just the one letter

Nothing more

Just k

Not even a capital

Just one tiny little letter all by itself

k

Shelly had sent a series of text messages pouring out her heart to a friend

She asked if they could meet and talk about it

And all she got back was

k

Not an OMG, or tell me more, or I can't believe it

No, just k

Shelly had expected more of a reaction

She didn't get anything but a k

And she was crushed

The confessions I hear from clients, who find comfort on the brown leather couches behind the closed doors of my office, might embarrass, shock, or alarm you. But what might surprise you even more are the numbers of adolescents I counsel who are deeply hurt by misinterpreted text messages. Then, add the number of parents I see who are propelled into panic mode by messages they misunderstand while monitoring their children's online exchanges; and, from where I sit, I see all sorts of problems that could have easily been avoided given the proper context.

What you type in a text or on Facebook, in a chat room forum or gaming exchange, and how someone perceives what you have typed, are often very different from what was intended. When your words are in print, rather than spoken with inflection, what your mind may believe is a complete thought can easily leave the other person lacking in interpretation. There are endless examples of what kids can come up with when they're trying to invent their own language. Just so you don't think I'm making this stuff up, we referred to webopedia.com to show you a few examples. "E" in a text message stands for Ecstasy...unless of course you're chatting it up with a gaming partner and then "E" represents the Enemy. You can see where context is key in that particular conversation. It's fairly easy for the most non-technically minded person to figure out *"2"* is the meaning for "to" and "4" takes the place of "for." Many people, regardless of how text savvy, could understand "2moro" or "4gvn", but would you know the meaning of LH6, or LHSX, if you saw it on your kid's phone? They both represent "Let's have sex!" The average parent might see RUMOF and assume it has something to do with drinking alcohol. But what it means to the current generation is, "Are you male or female?" If your child is posing that question to someone who has their phone number, it most definitely warrants a closer look. If you see RYB, you might be pleased. It stands for Read Your Bible. But a close cousin is RYO, or "Roll Your Own."

If your kids have memorized the majority of the list, they shouldn't have any trouble with textbooks. So, don't let them tell you their algebra assignments are 2M2H.

Will's mother frequently hears him use the term, *"That's what she said."*

So when she found the TWSS abbreviation online, she thought she would show it to him.

In her mind, he was going to laugh and think she was hip and cool for finding it and realizing it exists.

Instead, he picked up his iPad, and tapped on the Big Button Box APP.

On a red and yellow stripped background, there were the capital letters TWSS.

Anytime Will wants to say the phrase, he can just push a button and the iPad will say it for him.

Since his mom was doing her best to keep current, it was a bit disheartening for her.

Will rolled his eyes in recognition that his mom just doesn't get it.

But then on the very same page, she saw the numbers "143" and "1432."

Will's mom recognized those immediately.

"I love you" and "I love you too."

The numbers had represented those words since she was in her early 20's.

At least something has stayed the same.

Context is crucial if you are going to keep up with your teenager's texting, or if your child is going to avoid the pitfalls of perplexing electronic communications. When you don't know someone well, or you have doubts about how well you know them, it's easy to second guess something as simple as a text. A one-letter response like "k" can confuse even the most aware adult. Imagine what its capabilities are on the brain of an adolescent. It's easy to assume the person is being rude, is mad or just doesn't think enough of you to take the time to respond the way you expect. But in reality, they might have been driving, talking to someone else, or answering four other texts at the time yours came through, and they were trying to split their energy to answer all of them as expeditiously as possible. So, we have this new mode of communication that is quicker and more efficient in many ways, yet we are often left struggling with how to interpret a scaled down version of a conversation often taken out of context.

It's a precarious position for a parent diligently following up and screening messages sent and received on their children's phones. If you don't understand the vernacular or the context of the text, you are not going to interpret it correctly. And the divide that might already exist between parent and child becomes more of a cavern of miscommunication. If you interpret everything as concretely as the word that is written, you can quickly find yourself off course.

Davy and Angela were good friends.
She knew Davy was playing when he sent a text that read, *"Hey good lookin whatcha doing this weekend?"*
So she responded, *"I'm doing you, I hope."*

Davy shot back with, *"You couldn't handle me."*

At which point, Angela responded, *"I don't know why. All the other girls handle you."*

And on and on the texting went, back and forth, throughout the evening.

By the time it ended, they were both dosing off between messages.

Angela's mother found her daughter's phone on the bedside table still beeping from the last message.

Before she had read half of her 12-year-old daughter's texts, she was confident Angela was sexually active.

It's understandable that Angela's mother might assume her daughter is in a sexual relationship, if the text is read just as it is written. However, if you read it in context, in Davy's and Angela's vernacular, it's just funny. They are really good friends and they are joking around and actually being quite clever. The comments read sarcastically, and, read in context, are rather witty. But all of a sudden, we've got a parent who has read the messages verbatim and is freaking out trying to decide what to do, how to put a stop to it and how to forbid her daughter and this boy from having any further contact with each other. If she really knew her daughter or knew this young man, if she had ever been privy to their level of sarcasm, she might not have overreacted. But the mother-daughter relationship was already suffering when the incident occurred.

The lines are very much delineated in this parent-child relationship. There is not a lot of creativity or cleverness, and very little friendliness or humor, between the two of them. It's more of a *"go clean your room"* or *"do your homework"* authoritarian atmosphere in their home. Angela actually has a pretty cool personality which her parents don't often see. It's one of the frustrations of being a parent when you don't get to be party to some of the fun times. I frequently hear the complaint, *"Our children are so different around other people than they are with us."* In some instances that's just part of parenting. But on the other hand, you have to at least know a little something about the *"different child"* you perceive them to be around other people, in order to put their behaviors into perspective and correctly judge them.

There has to be room for open and honest conversations in your relationship as parent and child. It's not good enough to just sneak around and read their texts and emails or monitor their online search history. You also need to be having an active dialogue about the fact that you expect open access to their accounts. Even if you believe you know the context of your kid's conversations, it's not a good idea to view it secretly, so you can read what is being said. Chances are you're still not going to get the full story, and if they think you are going behind their back, then they're just going to shift modes of communication. I talk with these kids behind closed doors. I know what they are doing, and I know how they are trying to hide it. But don't despair. Most kids want boundaries. They will never admit it. They may fight and argue with you about it. But they really want to know where the lines are drawn, who is in charge, and who is in control. If they think it's them, their own security is threatened. They are kids.

If Angela and her mother had developed an open line of communication prior to the texting incident, Angela might have already told her mother about Davy. Her mother would have understood in advance that they were just friends, and that Davy was quick, clever and a bit sarcastic. As it unfolded, it was *"we caught you,"* now you're going to be punished. But then the parent's cover was blown for clandestinely checking future text messages. Angela ended up embarrassed and adamant that her parents would never meet her friend Davy. She's determined she'll find a way to be more secretive in her communications, and her parents are going to be less likely to find out the stuff that could be really dangerous down the road.

The text message Mark sent to Megan was simple enough and easy to understand.

"Do you want to study?"

Megan was asleep and didn't get the text until the next day.

She responded, "How about if we do it tonight?"

Mark quickly responded, "For real?"

And Megan sent back a text saying "Yeah, I've put it off for far too long."

After Mark replied, "I can't believe this, I've been waiting for a long time too," Megan was confused.

When she showed up at his house for their study session, Mark's parents were gone and he had something totally different in mind.

Dictionary.com defines the word ***context*** as "the parts of a written or spoken statement that precede or follow a specific word or passage, usually influencing its meaning or effect." So often with texting, especially with a generation developing its own electronic language, the words that should proceed or follow are no longer there. So, as parents and educators, we come again to the front lines with a decision to make. Do we only fight our battles to stay one step ahead of the possible pitfalls with technology and leave our children and students to fend for themselves? Or, do we prepare them in advance for cyber bombs?

Let's say you're the mother of a teenage girl who follows the pop-rock group, The Jonas Brothers. You think these Disney Channel movie stars are nice young men, and I'm sure they are. I'm also willing to venture out and say I may be taking the middle brother Nick's comment about texting out of context. But see what you think. *"When you're texting, you can say things to a girl that you'd never say in person. You just type what you want and press send."* Nick Jonas may have meant he would only say nice things to a girl and press send. But the spontaneity and the immediateness of a text, partnered with the loss of a complete language in its original context, can put even the savviest of texters in compromising situations. *"I was dating this guy and we would spend all day text messaging each other. And he thought that he could tell that he liked me more because he actually spelt (sic) the word 'YOU' and I just put the letter 'U."* Take it from Ozzy Osbourne's daughter, Kelly, many of today's relationships, our children's friendships, and their young love lives, are teetering on the edge of the next text.

Martha needed help and she didn't feel like she could talk with her mother.

Her mom had seemed angry a lot lately and Martha didn't want to risk making her mother mad.

Raised in the Catholic Church, Martha had been taught she could always contact the priest.

He was a family friend, and hip enough to know how to text, so Martha decided to give it a try.

Just minutes after she typed out her problem she received a response.

"Are you asking me what you should do, or are you asking God what you should do?"

Martha interpreted the text to mean, "You should be praying about this and not bothering me with it."

She responded with a rash reply, leaving her priest confused.

But he chose to overlook her abrupt comment and carried on with his day.

Later, when she saw him face-to-face, she was embarrassed to learn he was simply trying to clarify her text.

He really didn't know if she was asking a rhetorical question or actually wanted his personal opinion.

There is no doubt we all communicate better in person. It may not be as easy as texting, it may not give us the safety net we would like to have when saying something we wouldn't dare say to someone's face, but it does give us context. We can see the expression. We can hear the tone of voice. We can determine if there is sadness, boredom or laughing. We can see why a response may be taking longer than we thought it should. I'm not advocating you toss out your kid's cell phones and do away with all your texting. I text plenty of messages myself. It's very advantageous in a busy office where I may only get a couple of minutes between clients. But we've gone from primarily talking in person, or on the phone, to emailing, texting and tweeting. We are all readily trading over a million words in the English language for a few characters and symbols to mean what we say, while hoping we say what we mean.

Texting is not just precarious by nature of lost context, it has also introduces new social dilemmas such as drunken texting, sleep texting and text addictions. There are all sorts of studies currently underway for the ailments suffered by the chronic texter. The medical profession is already fielding complaints about neck, shoulder and spinal pain that doctors believe are a direct result of too much texting. There is even a new catch phrase out there; *"I love you like a teenager loves texting."*

The mass consumption alone should raise our eyebrows, grab our attention and interest us enough to open up a new dialogue with our children. Let them know you will have access to their phone. There doesn't need to be any secrets. You don't have to be rude or intrusive just because you're the parent. A healthy relationship will go a long way when it comes to openness and honesty between you and your children. Let your children know you are aware of the devices, websites and programs that not only teach, but encourage them to hide what they are doing on the phone and online. Let them know they can come to you with questions, and without fear. Help them understand the magnitude of context. A person's perception is their reality until they discover they have perceived a situation incorrectly. In some cases, it may be too late. A text message taken out of context can prompt a hormonal adolescent to make foolish decisions. A relationship ruined because of a quick, spontaneous reply is hard to repair.

This generation is up against obstacles we encounter ourselves. And yet, we. as adults. still fall victim to emails where we add our own inflection. Our spouses can be caught off guard when a text doesn't read exactly as it was written. And an employer can quickly become concerned when an employee doesn't answer the company cell phone during off hours. Imagine how an unanswered call affects your 16-year-old son when he's trying to phone his girlfriend, how a "TTYL" might be interpreted by a 13-year-old girl who just contacted her best friend looking forward to an evening of texting, or how a 15-year-old might misinterpret an email of "You drive me crazy", which was intended to be humorous. It's a lot to process for anyone, much less a child or a teenager.

Shelly didn't talk to her friend for several days.

When they would pass in the hall at school, Shelly looked away or acted like she was talking to someone else.

Finally her friend had the courage to ask her face to face what was wrong.

Shelly told her how offended she was, when she really needed to talk to her friend, and all she got back was a "k"

Her friend felt terrible.

But at least she had a chance to explain.

When Shelly's text message came in that night, she was sitting at the dinner table with her family.

Her Dad asked her to turn her phone off while they were eating and she was lucky to be able to tap out the "k"

By the time she got to school the next day and tried to explain, it was too late.

Chapter 10

We aren't in Kansas anymore

It should have been one of the most memorable nights of their lives.

The three couples had been friends for four years and tonight was their night.

They had the tuxes, the dresses, the limo and the dinner reservations.

When they arrived at the five-star restaurant, they were escorted to one of the best tables.

Drinks were served, dinner was ordered and the phones came out.

Sara was texting Brittany who was at a restaurant across town.

Alex sent a message to his parents promising to go straight to the prom after dinner.

Mackenzie was talking back and forth with her sister who wanted every detail of the big night.

All six of them were on their phones, yet no one was talking.

And it was Senior Prom night.

The Millennial Generation has never known life without technology. They move in social circles that exist within online communities and text more often than they actually talk. It seems they are more "connected" now than they have ever been in their lives. But in reality, they are becoming more isolated.

Humans are social animals. We need each other. A baby left without nurturing will die. We depend on each other for basic needs as well as encouragement and success. And as developers look at new and innovative ways to design the latest electronic gadgets, they are counting on our inherent need for reinforcement. Our need to be wanted, accepted, and applauded plays right into the ping, ding and the vibration of that next incoming message. Comedian Ellen DeGeneres understands exactly what I'm saying; *"I'm on the patch right now. Where it releases small dosages of approval until I no longer crave it, and then I'm gonna rip it off.*

It's in our nature as human beings to laugh at things that make us uncomfortable. But we've got to take a serious look at our priorities. There is no debating the fact that when you take your eyes away from the person standing in front of you and cast them down toward the cell phone that just vibrated in your hand, the person reaching out to you electronically has taken priority status in your life.

We know the people who are with us, like us. Don't we? We can be fairly safe in assuming they do. They choose to spend time with us, live with us or hang out with us. So if we are already with them, as the teenagers were on prom night, then that frees us up to find out who else might like us, want to communicate with us or spend time with us electronically.

Even though self-esteem is how we measure our own self-worth, it is frequently tied up in how we think other people view us. No one has probably ever said it better, or been more famously known for putting it all out there, than Academy Award winning actress Sally Field, when accepting her 2nd Oscar for Best Actress. *"The first time I didn't feel it. This time I feel it. And I can't deny the fact that you like me. Right now, you like me!!"*

Facebook and other similar forms of social media provide our children with a platform to be liked, to *"be somebody."* As you may very well know, *"going viral"* on YouTube doesn't mean the flu is spreading across the school campus. And even a crowd of adults, all standing around a coffee shop texting, can look important and impressive. We're not only witnessing this form of behavior, we're modeling it.

There was one problem on the 6th grade math worksheet that Bobby didn't understand.

"Mom, can you come over here and look at this? I don't get it."

"Give me one second, Bobby," his mom responded. "Let me return this text."

As Bobby sat at the kitchen table waiting, his mom returned several text messages.

"Mom, are you coming?" he asked as he watched 15 minutes go by on the stove clock.

"Yes, baby, I'll be right there, I promise. This is important. This is work stuff."

Bobby waited for another 30 minutes, then put his worksheet in his folder and went to his room.

On the way to school the next day, she asked him about his homework.

He told her he had figured it out on his own.

But she wasn't really listening.

She was pulling the car over on the side of the road to respond to another text.

Author and philosopher Vernon Howard said, *"A truly strong person does not need the approval of others any more than a lion needs the approval of sheep."*   The texting, Twittering and Facebooking is an esteem issue.

I believe we are coming out of a time in recent history where there was so much discussion about self-esteem and self-worth that people really got tired of talking about it.

But in reality, we need to talk about it more than ever because self-esteem is what is at stake here. The way we view ourselves and the way our children see themselves, has to balance out this constant pressure to be present at all times. It used to just be at work or school. Now it's at work, it's at school, it's in our relationships, it's on our phones, the iPad, and the computer. Everyone is sending messages and expecting responses in a very specific way. When was the last time you felt anxiety because you were in a situation where it took time to return an electronic message? Just the idea that someone is on the other end anticipating your immediate response can bring on stress. We have to know how to set response boundaries and be able to teach our own children, and children in our schools, to do the same. How can our children develop a real sense of self if they are constantly playing into the hands of the expectations of others?

Even when we are asleep we can hear the phone buzz or we can hear it ding. I have a 17-year-old client who told me about responding to a 3 a.m. text. "I heard the ping and I just knew that I needed to respond and so I responded." When I asked him why he would wake up at that time of the morning to text a friend who was probably drunk and wouldn't even remember the typewritten conversation, he said, "Because they needed me." I will tell you the same thing I told this teenage boy. If you don't set boundaries, people will bulldoze their way into your life. Once they feel they can control you, you run the risk of being emotionally bullied by their expectations.

We're all in our own little technology bubbles. We have our screen time. We have our text time. We have our public personas and our online personas, but where is the average real self? And how does the way we project ourselves publicly affect other people? How are we affected by the way we perceive others via text, email and on social networks?

Kay is a former beauty pageant winner who hoped the experience would look good on her resume.

She's a recent college graduate and spends most of her time still searching for that dream job.

In a tough economy, her marketing degree has yet to land her a steady income.

So when she's not looking for work, or walking the dog, she will occasionally log on to Facebook.

Kay says she finds herself more depressed by the time she logs off.

While she's struggling to pay the bills on her small starter house, it seems her classmates are all succeeding.

Facebook is an exhibition of the homes, the cars and the exotic vacations.

Not so long ago Kay was chosen as the most beautiful and talented beauty queen among dozens of competitors.

But now she struggles with her self-esteem.

In the field of psychology, we've being dealing with this issue for a long time.

Trying to understand our perception versus what is really going on from other perspectives is reality testing and it almost has to be constant reality testing. I think women, specifically, are more susceptible to this, and not being satisfied with oneself is a core issue, one of the sub tests on eating disorder inventories. It's a susceptibility of comparison with others. One of the things that can happen to many of us is that we are taught to compare ourselves to those around us and to fit into this comparative kind of a situation. When we begin to turn inward and judge ourselves by the success of others or by how they look, or dress, it has one of two effects. It will likely leave us feeling better or worse. There is seldom any middle ground. But even so, we compare ourselves with people at school, work, in our neighborhoods and even at church. It's why magazines, movies and TV shows impact young people so much. It affects older people too, but specifically the young, because they think what they see is reality. It's the perception that everybody looks like the people in the magazines. Well, no, they don't. In fact, they don't even make up one percent of the population. The pictures we see are not real. Most often they are airbrushed or completely created by digital devices. But even when the pictures are real and not digitally enhanced or airbrushed, the people being photographed make up, again, less than one percent of the population.

As I meet with clients and listen to what they are telling me, I believe this same principle is at play in social networking. You have to have esteem to be able to look at what people are posting on Facebook and realize, okay, there are some people who have more than I do. There are some people who don't. You have to recognize that you probably don't pay as much attention to those who don't have as much as you do, but you pay more attention to those who appear to have more.

The need to be liked, approved of and accepted is the driving force behind many a Facebook post. Let's say a friend goes to Hawaii and they begin posting their photos on Facebook. It might be the "trip of a lifetime" so they're going to keep posting pictures on Facebook for about three months. But in your mind it's like, "Oh, well they're going to Hawaii every week…they're practically living in Hawaii… how long were they in Hawaii?" It may have been just a four day cruise where they climbed off the boat, spent half a day, shot some great photos and off they went. It's the perception you have of their life being better than yours that affects your self-esteem. It's a core issue that's not caused by the technology. The technology is just the vessel that brings it up to a priority position in your way of thinking. When we perceive others as having more or being more successful, we tend to put pressure on ourselves to rise to that level. We look around at all the demands already placed on us in society and believe that others expect us to   achieve the same success.

Whatever we can do as parents and educators to replace those unrealistic expectations with realistic expectations is where we can effect significant change. It's much like studies I've been involved with on college campuses where we used social norming to help prevent alcohol abuse. Instead of ignoring the fact that some college kids are going to drink, or trying to sweep it under the campus rug, we would publish the real drinking and partying statistics associated with that particular school at the beginning of the year. It let the students know, statistically, what was normal on their campus versus what they might have heard or perceived as normal.

A recent NPR story detailed similar research at the University of Virginia in Charlottesville. The university had 20,000 students enrolled when a study was conducted on drinking habits. Researchers found that, out of every one hundred students, 27 of them didn't drink at all. One-third of the students considered themselves moderate drinkers consuming one to three per occasion, but not every night. And only 20 students considered themselves to have a drinking problem.

Sociologists and psychologists found out years ago that a common misunderstanding among kids is that everyone goes to a college party to get wasted. But, actually, the research proves that belief to be false. The majority of students in attendance at a college get-together, where alcohol is being served, drink in moderation. The ones who expect everyone to get wasted are usually the only ones who overindulge. The kids who think getting drunk is accepted as normal, also believe they are expected to conform. That's the research. And it's consistent research. By combatting misperceptions with the reality of the research, the mindset is more likely to become that getting drunk is what is inappropriate rather than widely accepted.

Byron has propelled his ability to be the high school class clown into an envious Twitter account.

It's not unusual for most of the student body to violate Internet usage policies just to check his latest tweet.

Even with Twitter's 140-character limit, Byron has a knack for making people laugh.

It's who he is, it's how he is known, and it's where he gets his greatest approval.

But Byron has a problem.

He's not the only funny guy in school.

Once the other guy caught on to Byron's online popularity, he started sending out his own tweets.

The other guy's account has grown so fast, Byron suspects he's paying for followers.

He can't prove it, but it seems to be the only possibility that makes sense to him.

Now, he has to decide.

Does he continue enjoying the free forum for making people laugh?

Or does he pay $59 to a website that promises 15,000 new followers?

If Byron is going to pride himself on the number of followers hanging on to his every joke, then he has to have the number he wants or at least the actual number of people he says are following him. He can't lie, because anybody can go to his site and see how many followers are on there. Remember, this is a young teenager whose self-esteem and self-worth are completely caught up in how many people are watching his every word. He values himself by what others think of him and say about him. But now there's this unexpected dilemma. If he pays for followers, he can't let anyone know that he's paid. In his mind, it would be a lame thing to do. He doesn't want to appear lame or he's likely to have fewer followers. Who would want to follow someone they don't admire?

While Byron's biology teacher is in front of the classroom giving instructions on the next animal to be dissected, Byron is sitting in the back agonizing over what to do next about his Twitter account. I don't make this stuff up. These are the issues facing our children. Byron doesn't just worry about his number of followers and the competition that has ensued with his classmate, but he's also dealing with the expectations of those already signed on to his account. He has thousands of followers and they expect something witty. So there is a very real demand on him. The pressure of "OMG I've got to respond, I've got to respond, I've got to respond!! How am I going to respond?" Who do all these people expect him to be? I take into account that Byron has fed into their expectations of him, but now, who will feed the beast?

If you do a quick search of "Facebook Likes Tied to Self-Worth" you're likely to get a hit on an August 26, 2012 comic strip from joyoftech.com "poking" fun, yes, pun intended, at how we view ourselves through the online approval of others. Remember Comedian Ellen DeGeneres' quote about being on the approval patch? We frequently joke about things that make us uncomfortable. If our children are posting personal things about themselves, their thoughts, who they are hanging out with, where they plan to go, and the reactions are a series of "Likes" or 'thumbs up", then all is well in Mayberry. But what does happen when no one responds, or, for instance, your YouTube video gets a "thumbs down"? From a theoretical perspective, one of the things I know in psychology is that dichotomies are dangerous. The "thumbs up" or "thumbs down" is black or white. There's nothing in the middle. You can add a comment, but it's quicker for people to click "up" or "down". And how that translates for most people, even those who refuse to admit it, is an instantaneous twinge of approval or disapproval. It becomes who they are and not what they said or the picture they posted. It's dangerous. You see, what I'm saying is that the world is in the middle, and almost nothing is truly black and white; some would say nothing is black or white. But now, if you're a really loyal Facebook follower, you're almost forced into this "up" or "down" decision about everything. You get a dichotomy. It's either I'm supporting your comments or I'm not. And that's not a healthy place. It's not a healthy world to live in if everything is one way or the other.

I don't see any dialogue about the division of the "Like" and the "Dislike". But I can tell you from talking with some of the kids that I counsel, they are getting reinforcement for themselves by liking other people's comments or, more often, seeing others "Like" theirs. It becomes even more dangerous when you consider what happens if they don't get that reinforcement. When a child, or even an adult for that matter, gets their self-esteem or self-worth from an avenue of social networking, it often creates a pattern of negative behavior.

The new Facebook account was exciting for Brooke.

She had lost a lot of weight since high school and couldn't wait to reconnect with her old friends.

But after the initial barrage of "Welcome to Facebook" messages subsided, she seldom heard from anyone.

Even the "Friend Requests" were few and far between.

Then late one night, she posted how her boyfriend had mistreated her.

And the responses poured in.

The next night she wrote about having a migraine headache.

And there were a few sympathizers.

This continued night after night until only one or two people were left to respond to her rants.

But she still liked seeing what they would have to say.

I think what happens is people create a Facebook identity, or an online profile, and it broadens to other social media, but it's almost like they get caught in these patterns of responding, acting or thinking like the person they have created themselves to be. Or they get online at a specific time of day or night when they're feeling a certain way. You can literally see patterns develop.

One young man, who came to me for advice, was only going on Facebook at night. It was the best time for him to log on after school and after his homework. But it was also the time when he was tired and frustrated, and instead of remembering the positive things that had happened in his day, he was more focused on what had gone wrong. As I began to scroll down through his postings over a period of time, I was able to show him that 18 out of 20 things he had put up on Facebook were negative. It was stuff like who didn't treat him right that day, or who didn't do something he needed them to do. It was only a snippet in time when he was feeling this way, but it just happened to be the time when he was on Facebook. It was a dangerous place to be and certainly didn't feed into his need for positive feedback. Those who were responding to him were the ones who wanted to get in the gutter too. And that's something, as parents, we have to be very careful with, when allowing our children to get any type of online support. I think of it as an online locker room. When you go into a sports locker room, there's this expectation that people are hanging out telling stories, joking around, laughing and cutting up. It's not unusual or unexpected that the dialogue might eventually migrate to a low level. It's the same thing that often happens in online forums or when people respond to a negative comment with a negative comment. The boundaries are taken down when you aren't face to face. When the "in-person" social experience is removed, you can't always count on the fact that there will be social accountability. We've gotten better about cyber bullying and situations where people will start to call others out, but most people tend to avoid conflict. So what happens is, when you go on line and there's conflict, when it's in written form and you can view it, most people will brush over it and move on to something else. But unfortunately, someone will almost always stay around to feed the beast. If your child is posting something negative, then other people who are feeling the same way, or who get attention from their negative posts, will start commenting or egging them on, and then your child's self-esteem and self-worth end up on the altar of public opinion.

There is an intensity out there in the electronic world like we've never experienced before in our history. Some of the kids that I work with who are new adapters are getting away from Facebook because it's not fast enough. They are telling me they think Facebook is something you go to once a day, after school, and you post something, but it's slow. The response time, the feedback and the immediacy of it are actually very low. What they are shifting to is Twitter and "Twitter like" sites where it's snap, snap, snap, comment, and response, comment and response, back and forth in real time. But what happens is they risk losing even more of their meaning in the context of their conversations. If they are responding in the moment, responding in the immediate and not taking any time, then they're reacting out of emotions more than they are on thought. It takes time to think about things. And unfortunately, in many cases, our kids are no longer thinking for themselves. A Wi-Fi signal, not unlike an umbilical cord, is tying them to what others say, think and do. If we as parents and educators are not the ones telling them they have what it takes, if we are not the ones encouraging them to step up higher, if we are not modeling moderate behavior for them, someone online is going to show them a different way. Sometimes, it's just a matter of showing them there is a choice.

The young man who had fallen into a pattern of posting negative comments late at night would wake up the next morning after a good night's sleep, and he was feeling fine, at least for a while. He would go about his day and try not to think about his online reputation. When I showed him the comments he had made night after night, he was able to understand how he was the one providing the information other people were using to judge him. And all along he had been using their responses to gauge his self-worth.

We are raising the Facebook nation. We cannot allow our children to be set adrift online with no life rafts or anchors. We are responsible for this generation. What happens to them will be a reflection of how well we have prepared them, unless we leave them living in a bubble, unable to think for themselves.

Affectionately called "the father of motivation", Dr. Wayne Dyer, an internationally renowned author and speaker in the field of self-development, says, "Self-worth comes from one thing…thinking that you are worthy." Our children are worthy and we're the ones who need to convince them. Technology allows us to be connected with our children 24 hours a day. Our parents didn't have that luxury. But we must all keep it in context and never allow our electronic devices to become excuses for our real relationships. Regarded as the "mother of family therapy," the late Dr. Virginia Satir once said, "Every word, facial expression, gesture, or action on the part of a parent gives the child some message about self-worth." Your children can't see your expression when you text them. They can't understand your gestures if you are communicating with them through an email. You may have posted a thousand happy family photos, but if there is no real happiness in your home, the photos are just pixels on a page.

You can call it a coincidence, but when this sort of wisdom comes from the "father of motivation" and the "mother of family therapy", we might want to sit up and pay attention to this parenting advice.

Chapter 11

If It's All Uphill From Here,
We Will Need To Change Gears

The first day in a camping area without cell service was just weird.

Every time he thought about telling someone something, he tried to text.

But then the "No Service" alert would pop up on his phone and he would be reminded.

The second day he only reached for his phone a half dozen times.

The third day he left it in his room.

The fourth day his mom drove him into town where he could talk all he wanted.

But by then, he was so busy laughing with those at dinner he never even thought about his phone.

The fifth night he turned his phone off.

And much to his surprise he never even missed it.

Getting away for the weekend or taking a two-week vacation used to actually mean getting away and taking a break. But now, when we go away, our cell phones, laptops and iPads go with us. If phones aren't answered, text messages not returned or emails responded to, it throws people into a panic. Even some employers feel it necessary to be electronically connected to their employees 24/7. And gone are the days when a kid could rest up and recover on an occasional sick day. Now, teachers can send homework right through cyberspace and into the inner sanctum, heaping homework in the middle of the healing process. We just can't seem to escape.

While electronic technology has given us an outlet for communicating in places where once we were silent, there is some truth to the old saying that silence is golden. It is often in silence where we gather our thoughts, prepare our minds and really engage in the process of express learning.

When school let out for the summer, Ezekiel had high hopes for quickly completing all reading assignments.

He wanted to rest and relax without Summer Reading hanging over his head.

But here it was just a couple of weeks before the fall semester and he had procrastinated.

1066 The Year of the Conquest was the book he had to read for Honors History.

He went to the library with good intentions but quickly took a break to play a game on his iPad.

When his mom glanced over she saw a series of digital cars and guns moving rapidly across the screen.

She urged Ezekiel to return to his book and he did.

But after reading only a few words, he looked at his mother and said, "I can't understand it. I just can't get it."

It's not just an excuse Ezekiel is giving his mother in order to somehow avoid his summer reading assignment. There is a real physiological reason why he can't seem to make the words make sense. He was a rising 9th grader at the time, but I hear the same arguments from most of the college students I counsel. When your brain is being bombarded in a receptive learning situation, it has to slow down before it can shift into a mode of express learning. In order to focus in on each page of a book, and be able to learn the information that you need to learn, your brain has to have a chance to relax and change gears.

One of the key components that I analyze and conceptualize when I work with families and educators is express learning versus receptive learning. Receptive information is just information that we absorb. When we watch television, for example, that is receptive. Basically, you don't have to engage. All you have to do is turn it on and any information coming from the TV just washes over you. Regardless of what you might think you retain, you actually absorb a high percentage of it. One of the best ways I know to explain it is what happens in many of our homes every morning.

We turn on the TV and it seems to be mostly noise in the background. We're not really watching it, but as we move from room to room, we can still hear it. We may have it tuned to a news channel and, as the programming progresses, we might hear a weather report. Now we know whether or not rain is expected. Or we might hear if the traffic is bad so we know to avoid a particular area on our way to work or school. It's receptive. We are not engaged. We're not sitting there glued to the screen, watching each story as it unfolds. We're just retaining little tidbits of information. It's just knowledge we receive. We don't have to do anything except pay a little bit of attention and accept it. "Oh, it's going to be 105 today."

Express knowledge is when we actually have to engage. It's quality versus quantity. This is the type of knowledge that we not only retain but also benefit from in brain growth. When we actively engage, we're able to really learn something. The example I use with college students is that there is a difference between listening to the radio or watching TV and reading a textbook. Watching TV is a receptive process; reading a textbook is a very expressive knowledge process. Your brain operates at two different levels. In the receptive mode, which I refer to as the fast speed, you can be doing eight different things at once. If my wife Lisa is in the kitchen cooking breakfast, she can also be telling the kids to get their clothes on and brush their teeth, while she's simultaneously texting her assistant to postpone an appointment at work. She can still hear on the television that it's raining and recognize she needs to grab an umbrella. Students understand this analogy because they are also used to multi-tasking. But you can't do eight different things and read a textbook. Lisa would encounter the same obstacle if she walked straight into her office and picked up the latest research on psychotherapy. It takes time to transition. And as we move further into our new world of technology, we're going to have to recognize how and when it's necessary to change gears.

Roger's parents felt certain he had some sort of a learning disorder.

He had made average grades in high school that were good enough to get him into a small community college.

But half way through his freshman year, he was failing.

"The information just doesn't go into my head," he told his parents. "I sit down to try and read the textbook and I try to learn the stuff for the test but I can't do it. It just doesn't stick. I have read and re-read it and I still don't   remember   any   of   it."

Roger's parents encouraged him by telling him he was smart enough to do it.

But no matter what they tried, he was convinced there was something wrong with him.

And eventually he convinced them.

Out of ideas, they sought professional counseling for their son.

When I start investigating cases like Roger's, and when I start looking at the learning process he's using, it's not unusual to find technology at the base of the mountain he's trying to scale. He's got the textbook in front of him and open to the chapter he's supposed to be studying, but he's also returning a text to a guy down the hall in his dorm. The flat screen TV is on in the background and periodically there's a knock on his door when someone is hoping he'll take a break and go a couple rounds on Madden NFL 13 or Halo. So Roger decides to pack up and go to the library where it is quiet and he can study. He's got his iPod on listening to music as he heads across campus. He sees a few friends and stops to talk. Finally, he gets to the library, sees another group of friends and tells them he really has to study. He finds a cubicle, sits down, opens his book and begins to read. But nothing he reads seems to make sense, and he certainly isn't remembering any of it.

You have to find a way to get engaged and that takes time. You may have to experiment a little with what will work for you, but it's a step down process. Just like the young man going one week at a campground without cell service, it took time to disengage. Imagine your brain going 100 mph, but express knowledge only happens at 25 mph. You can't just pull the parking brake and stop a car. You have to gradually slow a car. Or think about our brain in terms of a boat. You can't just hit the brakes on a boat. It doesn't work. You've got to slow it down.

When I'm talking with students, I recommend a two-step process.

1) Get a magazine and start flipping through it. You don't have to read the articles, just look at the pictures. Gradually, what will happen is your eye will catch an article and it will slow your brain down a little. 2) Put the magazine away and pull out something fun to read. You will, logically, anticipate something positive if you already know it's something you enjoy reading. Encourage your children or students in your class not to go straight to the dry physics book. It's not going to work. Maybe they spend ten minutes flipping through a magazine and another ten reading something they enjoy. All they have lost is 20 minutes. But what they have gained in return is the next 40 minutes where they can study and actually learn something, because now their brain has shifted to express mode. They can recall the information because now they're actually absorbing it. Their brain is able to make the necessary connections because they are on a different wavelength.

Two weeks into the new school year, parents were invited to the high school.

The idea was to follow their child's schedule and meet the teachers.

Each teacher had planned a five-minute presentation.

But one teacher in particular got everyone's attention.

The Algebra teacher explained that the student's book and all other materials would be on computer.

They had a copy on their laptops, but in the event of a malfunction there was also a copy online.

If the students didn't understand a particular lesson, there were six online teachers explaining a similar lesson.

He told the parents their kids could review what they had learned and even pick the online instructor they liked best!

When it comes to technology, there's a distinct difference in receptive and expressive. The word being used in the field of technology is "engaged." Engaged technology is better. It's really no longer good enough just to have technology; it has to be engaged technology. It has to be something where the students are learning something and engaged in the process of learning, rather than just spending time. Again it goes back to the factors of learning. It's not enough just to have exposure. It has to be quality over quantity, and it has to be engaged. A student must be paying attention.

The good news for students trying to learn in a world fraught with technology is that companies are still recognizing the value of meeting a need. Since we're all crunching data and getting data thrown at us at rapid-fire speed, it's hard to find the time to slow down enough to truly engage. So, many of the companies are making things as user friendly and fast as possible. It's the way our brains have been going and if developers can't make people understand the technology then they will make the technology understand us.

The textbook is inherently boring. Hopefully, the textbook your child has to read is well written and makes a good cogent argument, which is less boring. But, in general, textbooks are a lot of words that don't have nice beautiful pictures to see and motivate you to read more. It's information. It's just raw information. What the textbook companies are trying to do is take the information and make it more interactive. It's engaging students a little more rather than having them work harder to understand it. There's a real upside to that type of changing technology. It makes books more fun. It makes books easier to read. It offers a receptive way to engage in the learning process.

But as parents and educators, we also have to recognize what's at stake when we simplify the method. It does affect our children's ability to go back to an old school process, slow their brains down, and read raw data. Very few people read raw data anymore. There are students out there still trying to have original thoughts and original conversations while looking at things in new, innovative and original ways. But it's rare. Most kids are now just accepting other people's interpretation of everything. When things are user friendly, it means the information has been processed. It's been statistically broken apart, copied, divided and maximized for what is going to be the quickest way to distribute the information. It does not mean it's the best way.

Let's say I have twenty different points I'm trying to make. But I know the average reader is only going to read seven. You see it all the time on bookshelves and articles in magazines. Sometimes you hear it from the pulpit of your local church. There are five ways to do this, or seven great solutions for that, or six great new dieting tips. But does it mean there are only that many? The self-help book, Seven Habits of Highly Effective People, has sold millions of copies worldwide. Does that mean there are only seven? Really? There's only seven? No, there's actually a lot more than seven but that's all the average person is going to read. It even makes for a good title. But what we get is processed information.

It's great to be able to type a topic into a search engine on the computer and get a quick answer. But the problem it presents is that very few people are reading the material in its entirety. It's easy to stay informed if you can pick up the news in snippets. USA Today was one of the first papers to give us world news in a paragraph. It's much faster for all of us to glance at the ticker moving along the bottom of the TV screen tuned to CNN so we don't have to watch news for the rest of the day. Of course, we can also Google the headlines or click on Yahoo to see what they think are the top ten news picks of the day.

As parents and educators, if we can go back in time and think about how we learned to engage, how we learned to write, and how we learned to think about things, then we start to recognize how drastically our society is changing directions. I believe what we are doing now is sometimes robbing kids of the ability to figure how to engage, how to think at that lower and slower level. If they don't ever develop the ability to do that, all they are doing is just absorbing other people's information. They won't be able to get to that next level of creating, designing and inventing new things. In some ways, they are losing the ability to think for themselves.

It had been a couple of years since the Alexander family had taken a vacation.

The timing still wasn't exactly right so they decided to go ahead and book a weekend getaway.

It was a three-hour drive to their destination.

The morning they left, Adam, the 15-year-old, started his day with two hours of television.

He spent the next two hours on the road playing with his iPad.

When his mom asked him to put it away, he got on his cell phone.

When she demanded that he spend some time thinking or looking out the window, he obeyed.

About five minutes later, when she turned around to look again, he was playing with the GPS.

It seemed absurd to Adam for his mother to require him to look out the window or spend time thinking when he could quickly pass the time with any number of electronic options. But what this 15-year-old doesn't yet understand is how the constant barrage of meaningless images puts his brain in neutral and could easily impact his long-term ability to create an original thought. Adam might be interested in the words of a man he will likely study in one of his high school science classes. Galileo said, "All truths are easy to understand once they are discovered; the point is to discover them."

We've got to give our children a chance to be the innovators, the designers, or developers, the ones who contemplate, create and invent. But in order to do this, we also need to focus on limiting their use of receptive technology.

Our children need and deserve more than information that is just absorbed by their brains. Video gamers often argue with me that their minds are engaged when they're playing because they've had to learn a skill in order to play the game. But I retaliate with the fact that, once they've learned the basic skills of the game, they're just along for the ride. It's another opportunity to make a car analogy, which they seem to understand. When you are first learning to drive a car you are most engaged in what you are doing. You are paying attention, your hands are at 10 and 2, you're shifting gears, and you're looking all around trying to figure out where you are going. The process has you completely engaged. But most driving involves going to the same places time after time. We drive to school, to work, to the shopping mall, to church, to homes of friends and family. There comes a point when we're no longer engaged. We're listening to the radio, we're driving the car, we're talking on the phone, we're texting, we're eating and drinking, we're doing all kinds of stuff. I can't tell you how many people say, "I don't even remember getting home tonight." They were disengaged, thinking about something else, receiving information but not retaining it. It's the same thing with video gaming. Once you've learned the skills, it fades back into a receptive process. You are now just following the levels and doing it over and over again rather robotically. It's entertaining, it's stimulating, but it's no longer engaging.

As we add more and more technology into our lives, into our homes and our schools, we've got to continue to engage the learning process and balance the amount of technology we use. All technology and all screen time are not bad. I'm not in any way advocating against electronic gadgets. As you can imagine, our family has its fair share. We just recently did some research on the types of technology we are using here in the office. Balancing out the difference in receptive and express knowledge is really going to be key.

We need to use the technology without allowing it to control our children or us. We all need quiet time, or step-down, time to regroup, refocus and avoid becoming a pawn in someone else's plan. Teenagers have a tendency to accuse their parents of trying to control them. You might try helping them understand that they will instead, be controlled by lifeless technology, if they refuse to moderate their own usage. Tony Robbins, self-help author and writer of the books, *Unlimited Power and Awaken The Giant Within,* puts it like this: "In essence, if we want to direct our lives, we must take control of our consistent actions. It's not what we do once in a while that shapes our lives, but what we do consistently."

As a psychologist, speaker, author, husband and dad, I recommend moderation in all things. It works for educators, parents and children. I predict we will see an even greater need for it as the next round of new technology takes us for a ride.

Chapter 12

If You're Happy and You Know It,
Your Facebook Will Surely Show It

She stood on the platform with her hands in the air.

Around her neck, two big gold plated medals swung back and forth on red, white and blue ribbons.

It wasn't the Summer Olympics but the tumbling state championships.

The star athlete, the state champion, was our four-year-old daughter, Taylor.

You could tell by the big smile on her face that she was happy.

She was really, truly, happy.

Her ipad was packed away in a gym bag, for this was not a moment she could have experienced electronically.

We were there with her, cheering her on and enjoying our own state of happiness.

The pictures, of course, are posted for all our friends on Facebook.

"Authentic happiness involves living a life full of appreciation - being mindful of each and every moment - and passionately pursuing knowledge, friendships, health and career goals." So go the words of Dr. Martin Seligman, a pioneer in the field of positive psychology, whose work and research has followed a pursuit of happiness. A past president of the American Psychological Association, Seligman took psychology, as a profession, in a whole different direction. Instead of pouring all of our energy into what's not good or what's not working, Seligman proposed studying what is effective and what is helpful. He pushed an agenda of positive psychology and eventually published a number of successful books on the topic.

What I remember was how it shaped my experiences as an undergraduate student in a pre-professional psychology program. It was a lot like pre-med, but for budding psychologists. We were assigned to do projects, in addition to our regular class assignments, and so I chose to work with my advisor to develop a new course of study on effective psychology. Because at that point there wasn't a textbook available, we had to delve into the research, and actually put the class together from scratch. I believe the experience had a great impact on my professional life. I try not to focus on what is wrong or what's not working in a client's life, but rather, recognize it's just as effective, and far more positive, to ask what is working and recommend they do more of it.

When Claire first sought counseling, she was having problems making friends.

As she talked, it became clear that her expectations were very self-focused.

She left little room for anyone's opinions or hobbies beyond her own.

But after a summer away from school, she came back with a different perspective.

As she watched other teenagers engaging in friendships at the beach, she observed a lot of give and take.

If one person wanted to build a bonfire, while the other wanted to go for a walk, they worked it out.

When a surfer wanted to catch waves, while his girlfriend wanted to lie in the sun, they compromised.

Claire confided that maybe she had been the reason for her own solitude.

But instead of focusing on what she had done wrong, Claire was encouraged to make it right.

She began opening herself up, offering invitations and accepting invitations.

When relationships began to develop, Claire started to realize that, in order to have friends, you have to be a friend.

It was important to identify the factors that had changed in order for her to understand and begin focusing on what did work, rather than what didn't. Claire could have spent countless hours in counseling going over everything that was negative in her life. But seeing the potential for friendships in a positive light rejuvenated and even motivated her to do things differently. Some psychologists might argue that you can end up with the same results by working through all that is bad…getting it out of the way…and then moving forward. I prefer a more positive perspective, setting aside what doesn't work and focusing on what actually does.

Mihaly Csikszentmihalyi is another great innovator who caught my attention early on in the study of human psychology. As a research psychologist at the University of Chicago, he did extensive studies in optimal peak experience. What he discovered is when people say they are the happiest, they frequently describe a state of being. It's a mindset where they seem to detach from a current awareness or current reality and get caught in this kind of peak performance or optimal experience. When people think about being happy, according to Csikszentmihalyi, what they are often describing is a moment in time, when everything seems to come together. The easiest examples to explain, perhaps not necessarily the best, are usually athletic.

Michael Jordan has described the experience as a laser-like focus. At the end of a game, he has said he knew the crowds were yelling and screaming and people were going crazy, but the only thing he could visualize, really see, or even think about was getting the ball into the basket. Rock climbers similarly have described a state of becoming one with the mountain by envisioning the handholds and footholds that would ultimately lead to their success. Likewise, chess players have described the moments when everything comes together, and they could actually see the moves that would lead them to victory in the game. This is how happiness is described.

Sandy was 51 years old when she finally lived out her childhood fantasy to barrel race.

Out west where she was raised, rodeos were the biggest annual events.

She would watch the contestants, in their shiny cowgirl clothes; ride as if they were one with their horse.

At night, she would lie in bed and drift off to sleep dreaming of what it would be like to be them.

Eventually, she would own her own old barrel horse, but she was only eleven and never got a chance to race.

So she just continued to dream.

Her horse was sold.

And her life changed course.

Then, long after most people would have given up on the idea, she actually got the chance.

A cowboy let her borrow his horse.

Several people gathered around to give her advice, including a barrel racing champion and a rodeo queen.

Sandy says all she could see was the horse and the next barrel.

And as she turned to make the final fast run, she realized it felt exactly how she had always dreamed it would.

Despite all those watching, she couldn't hold back the tears as she described how happy she felt.

Csikszentmihalyi wanted to know more about this subjective reality people were describing, and so he set about doing a quantitative study on the qualitative experience. He broke it down and looked at the human brain as if it were a computer with a certain amount of processing speed.

On a regular basis, our brain is using only a small percentage of its ability to crunch information. So what he conceptualized, using the computer analogy, is when the computer processor in our brain is dedicating and processing the majority of its energy to one consistent thing, it locks in and there's no room for distraction. Whatever it is, you've got a goal and you're achieving it. He found that if you are solely focused on that positive experience or that huge accomplishment, you couldn't process negative things. And so, subjectively, real true happiness has been identified as that kind of experience.

What I try to help kids and parents understand, as I work with them through some of these issues and ideas, is that there is a difference between happiness and bliss.

I think one of the things we do, especially in our culture and our society, is we get mixed up and begin chasing pleasure rather than directing our focus to the things that would ultimately bring us genuine happiness. While happiness is a cognitive process that is goal oriented toward achieving something in a more positive direction, bliss, is basically associated with the release of neurochemicals in the brain. What we've begun to believe as a society is that happiness is about entertainment. The 70's model of happiness was sex, drugs and rock and roll. But in reality those were all pleasures. Those were all things that were temporary, chemical-induced, physical reactions to stimulus. As a result, we have confused happiness or true positive feelings with chasing these physiological experiences.

An example we're familiar within this age of technology is going to a movie. The reason why movies are getting bigger and louder with better sound systems and high definition images is to engage all the senses. The more endorphins are released during the experience, the more you can detach from reality for about 2 hours and 35 minutes. But that detachment is an endorphin-released buzz of pleasure, not a goal driven positive direction toward true happiness. It's much the same way as when you go to the fair and ride a roller coaster. The fast break straight downhill releases a central nervous system induced endorphin high. It leaves you feeling excited. But we wrongly interpret that excitement by generalizing it as happiness. It's not. Pleasure is producible and short term. It's a physiological reaction that doesn't last very long. It goes away. And if there's nothing positive, healthy or good behind it, then, when it's over, you're right back where you started. It's kind of like alcohol. You have a drink, and for the temporary time that the alcohol is being processed by your system, you're in a suspended state of reality. Your central nervous system is depressed, you're more uninhibited, and subjectively, you're feeling better than before. But then the alcohol is processed through your liver, and when it's gone, you have to have more, or you're left with whatever was there before you started drinking.

Happiness, on the other hand, is an experience that, because it's positively driven and goal oriented, it's sustainable. You can keep it longer and after the experience you have something to show for it that has actually changed you in a positive way. It's not a momentary experience. And as Helen Keller so eloquently shared with the world, it's not necessarily obtained by something you see or hear. "Happiness cannot come from without. It must come from within. It is not what we see and touch or that which others do for us which makes us happy; it is that which we think and feel and do, first for the other fellow and then for ourselves."

And, so, one of the things I always try to focus on in our practice is separating out and distinguishing that you can have bliss without happiness, or you can have happiness and still have bliss. Happiness and bliss together are the best ways I know to have your cake and eat it too. The bliss you feel when you're happy, actually feels better, and lasts longer. Even if you're going to chase pleasure, it's in your best interest to try and chase it when you are already happy.

Identifying and finding ways to focus on the positives, and to find those positive goals and those positive orientations, are the things I think we're losing in our society and our culture. Relating to technology, it can be used for those positive directions and goals, but more increasingly, it is being used simply as a vehicle for bliss. It's a distraction. It's entertainment. It's an endorphin buzz rather than something that is used for a positive, true, happy state of being.

Over 1400 people follow Bryson on Facebook.

Every day, many of them log on for the sole purpose of reading his latest post.

His words are always positive, uplifting and encouraging.

And, he frequently shares his family's happiest moments in photographs.

Although Bryson could easily pursue a profession as a motivational speaker, it's not what he does for a living.

He actually deals with death on a daily basis.

Bryson is a third generation funeral home director.

Surrounded by grieving families, he is compassionate and kind.

But Bryson's primary focus is being a light in the dark, and bringing joy to others when all seems lost.

Funny, he has found one of his greatest followings on Facebook.

If you were to search the Internet for ways to experience happiness, you would likely find more than you care to count. But after studying and practicing human psychology for several years, I've come to the conclusion, like many other psychologists, that there are only four primary methods leading to long-term happiness. Although I acknowledge technology can certainly be a tool, as Bryson uses it, nowhere in this list will you find an actual electronic device.

First, I believe true long-term happiness can be found in mutually respectful interdependent relationships. The kind of relationships you might have with a husband or wife or a dear friend, the kind of relationships that are give and take, healthy and ongoing.

Second, we typically experience happiness when we are doing something constructive that produces energy, rather than an activity that leaves us feeling drained. If you think of it like a bank account, then the goal would be to have more in the account at the end of your day than when you started. In other words, you are choosing to exert your energy in a way that allows you to feel better, because you're accomplishing something and seeing the end results.

Thirdly, people who give back describe themselves as happy. Again, using the example of Bryson, he's giving back by posting positive messages on his Facebook page. It's not necessarily the kind of giving we often associate with money; it doesn't have to be donating financially, but simply doing something selflessly for others. It truly is an act of encouraging someone by lifting them up with your actions, for example, opening a door, allowing someone to go next in traffic or letting another person skip ahead in the checkout line when they only have one item and you have a full cart. These are the types of things people have described doing when they felt they were genuinely experiencing happiness.

The fourth way I see people achieving true lasting happiness is when they are in relationship with a power greater than themselves.

To do any of these four takes time, energy and effort. And that means technology can, as I mentioned before, be a tool. But it can't be the end all to happiness. Technology will never produce lasting happiness in and of itself. It is, however, helpful if you want to text a loved one with who you are in a mutually respectful and interdependent relationship. Or an application like Skype or FaceTime can be used so we can actually see family members and friends who are too far away to visit. Technology can certainly help us at school and work to be more productive and efficient. We can also use technology to help others and give of ourselves in the process. And technology gives us a world of access to more religious text than we could have ever imagined. When I was growing up, I don't even think our library had copies of all the religious text. Now, at the touch of a button, just about everything that has ever been written on religion or spirituality is right before our eyes. But, it's just a vehicle. It's not actual happiness. It's a tool that will help you achieve happiness in a more efficient and better way. It's not the answer itself. It's where we often get confused and where our children are being led astray. For instance, is the ipad, the iphone, the Facebook page or the Twitter account helping us get from point A to point B, or are we mistaking these things as a point of destination? Children often associate the games they play, the posts they read, the chat lines they can access, as what makes them happy. But, as parents and educators, we have to help them understand these things are devices, not destinations. We love riding in cars; but the car is only a way to get from where we are right now, to a really cool location like the beach.

"We hold these truths to be self-evident, that all men are created equal, that they are endowed by their Creator with certain unalienable Rights, that among these are Life, Liberty and the pursuit of Happiness." Since the Declaration of Independence was signed in 1776, we have been in an all-out pursuit of happiness. In today's world of technology, we will not find a text, a Tweet or a game of Halo will accomplish this pursuit of happiness.

You've probably heard it said, it's smart to learn from your own mistakes but it is wise to learn from the mistakes of others. I think people who have had struggles in their lives have often worked through a combination of what doesn't work and what does. And, often times, they become more willing to listen to older, more experienced people who have travelled a similar path. In the course of analyzing what doesn't work, what does work and what lasts, they figure out how to experience real true happiness.

I find some of the happiest people on the planet are in Alcoholics Anonymous or in prisons. I'm not saying either one of those is a model for happiness. They certainly are not. But these are people who have explored all the things that didn't work. They've reached the bottom and begun searching for a real solution. Once they figure out, "All right I've pretty much tried everything that didn't work," then they decide to try and listen to other people and see what does work.

There was a time when Mike lived only for himself.

He didn't take time for family or friends but spent as much time as possible in pursuit of his own pleasures.

He looks back on it now and hopes he can help keep others from making the same mistakes.

It was a careless accident on his part that left Mike a quadriplegic.

He likes to tell how quickly he made amends with his Maker while he was lying there unable to move.

And, during the therapy that followed, he was able to identify his true friends and reunite with his family.

Mike, who once prided himself on being wild and free, is still confined to a wheelchair.

He doesn't have much access to all the latest technology.

But he is almost always smiling and now knows the sources of real true happiness.

It might be good to learn from what I've been able to tell you. But as we forge forward into our technology driven future, I believe it is wise to heed these additional words from Dr. Martin Seligman. "The good life consists in deriving happiness by using your signature strengths every day in the main realms of living. The meaningful life adds one more component: using these same strengths to forward knowledge, power, or goodness. A life that does this is pregnant with meaning, and if God comes at the end, such a life is sacred."

Technology can be used for those positive directions and goals, but more increasingly, it's become a means of distraction, rather than something that's used for a positive, true happy state of being. If you look at people who are addicted to drugs, many started out taking pills. The pills had to dissolve and filter through their body in order for them to obtain the high they were after. It took time and the addiction potential at that point was lower. But eventually they graduated to injecting the drug in a liquid form straight into their veins. It became highly addictive and far more dangerous. Technology is really a lot like that direct injection. It's fast, it's easy, it's affordable, but unlike a drug addiction, it's socially acceptable. When your 15-year-old looks at you now and says, "Everybody's doing it," she's far more right than we ever were, when we used that same excuse with our parents.

I'm using an extreme analogy here by comparing your child's ipad or laptop with drugs. But it works just as well to consider what happens when your child becomes so hooked on video games, and the game becomes the destination. Once the game is over, like when the high from a drug wears off, there is nothing positive underneath. So then your child is faced with, "What's next?" If there is nothing there that feels good, nothing that is better than how it felt to master that last level, then why not do another one? Since doing something productive that produces energy leads to happiness, then doing something unproductive that eventually drains you of energy is sure to lead your child toward unhappiness, guilt and depression.

Technology is not going to go away. We can utilize it for good or ignore its power and eventually find ourselves in a crisis. John F. Kennedy, the 35th President of the United States said, "When written in Chinese, the word "crisis" is composed of two characters. One represents danger and the other represents opportunity."

We have to acknowledge technology is now, the danger is real, and we can't afford to waste our opportunity. Our children have to be armed with the education they need. As a middle school teacher describes the situation, "You can still look across a classroom and pick out with some accuracy who will be the football player, the cheerleader, or the one to achieve academic excellence. But you cannot tell, with any certainty, which is in serious trouble with the technology entrusted to them." A young, popular teenage girl from a good family recently put it this way, "I can't really get away with doing drugs. And I can't really get away with drinking all that much. But, I can go into my room, shut the door and look at pornography. My parents don't have a clue. There's not even any danger of getting caught when I'm out. It's not like I'm going to be pulled over and given a sexalyzer test."

Looking for further answers –
Be watching for the follow-up book:

Digital Dieting: A New Model for Technology Consumption

And other exciting products and services

Follow us
www.StewartBeaversInstitute.com

Facebook:
www.facebook.com/StewartBeaversInstitute

Twitter: @ stewartbeaversinstitute

YouTube: The Stewart-Beavers Institute

Dare to Change

The real problem is not whether machines think but whether men do. ~ B.F. Skinner, *Contingencies of Reinforcement*, 1969